MW00629896

REVOLTING
RECIPES FROM
HISTORY

For Wendy Clark – thank you for the inspiring conversation about cellar rats over coffee and in memory of the late Alan Clark for all the times he stopped by the office and offered encouragement, wise words on life and a vegetarian sandwich to keep me going!

REVOLTING RECIPES FROM HISTORY

SEREN CHARRINGTON HOLLINS

PEN & SWORD
HISTORY

AN IMPRINT OF PEN & SWORD BOOKS LTD.
YORKSHIRE – PHILADELPHIA

First published in Great Britain in 2022 by
PEN AND SWORD HISTORY
An imprint of
Pen & Sword Books Ltd
Yorkshire – Philadelphia

Typeset in Times New Roman 12/16 by
SJmagic DESIGN SERVICES, India.
Printed and bound in the UK by CPI Group (UK) Ltd.

Pen & Sword Books Limited incorporates the imprints of Atlas, Archaeology,
Aviation, Discovery, Family History, Fiction, History, Maritime, Military, Military
Classics, Politics, Select, Transport, True Crime, Air World, Frontline Publishing,
Leo Cooper, Remember When, Seaforth Publishing, The Praetorian Press,
Wharncliffe Local History, Wharncliffe Transport, Wharncliffe True Crime and
White Owl.

For a complete list of Pen & Sword titles please contact
PEN & SWORD BOOKS LIMITED
47 Church Street, Barnsley, South Yorkshire, S70 2AS, England
E-mail: enquiries@pen-and-sword.co.uk
Website: www.pen-and-sword.co.uk

Or
PEN AND SWORD BOOKS
1950 Lawrence Rd, Havertown, PA 19083, USA
E-mail: Uspen-and-sword@casematepublishers.com
Website: www.penandswordbooks.com

MIX
Paper from
responsible sources
FSC® C013604

Contents

Introduction

What is a revolting recipe? When it comes to defining revolting food, disgust is not just a matter of taste. Disgust is a strong emotion defined by physiological and cognitive factors, but also by relational, social and cultural aspects. Our food choices are to a large extent determined by our upbringing and the cultural backdrop in which we are raised.

Food is our fuel and it is universally accepted that we need a ready intake of food in order to survive. Disgust is both ingrained within our culture and is also an evolutionary function to help us avoid disease and unsafe food, but whilst the need to eat is universal the foods we find disgusting are not. What is considered delicious or a delicacy to one person can be revolting to another.

So, when considering the question of what constitutes a revolting food then it all comes down to a matter of taste. The classification of 'disgusting' can be as varied as humankind itself. Indeed, the saying, 'One man's meat is another man's poison' has never been truer than when used to define disgusting food. In a 1905 newspaper article entitled, 'Decayed Food' the fickle attitude towards food in a 'state of partial decay' is explored:

> A fancy for food in a state of partial decay seems a morbid and unwholesome one, yet such a taste is found to exist in most parts of the world. Even in England we are partial to ripe Stilton and fragrant Gorgonzola; we like our game high and medlars rotten. In Russia a soup made of rotten cabbages, and known as schee, is a chief article of diet. To foreigners it is a very disgusting dish, the odour of

which clings to the dwellings in a "forget-me-not" style. And Sir Joseph Banks found that the South Sea Islanders were fond of decaying jelly-fish. "Though after they had eaten it," he adds, "I confess I was not extremely fond of their company."

Perhaps even more disgusting to our tastes is a favourite dish of the Alaskan Esquimaux. It is prepared in the following manner: raw salmon heads are packed in a hole in the ground and left in the sun for ten days. Being then in a lively condition, full of maggots, they are eaten greedily, and form one of the dishes always set before an honoured guest. The name of this item in their menus is triplicherat.

Is there any reason for these strange tastes, asks Health, or are these rotten meats eaten merely eaten to please the palate? There are two facts which, taken together, suggest a possible reason: 1) all decaying matter is full of bacteria; 2) bacteria are active agents in the digestion of food. It may be, then, that food in a state of incipient decay is taken as an aid to digestion. *(Barry Herald*, 17 February 1905).

It is certain that some foods are eaten not because they are delicious but because they are considered healthy, while other foods are considered unhealthy, but scrumptious. On the whole whether a food is considered healthy or unhealthy doesn't really factor into whether it is classified as revolting or not; it has more to do with culture.

Disgust is undoubtedly our defence mechanism, evolved to protect us against potentially harmful foods and other pathogens that lie at the root of our avoidance of certain foods. For this we draw on the long history of ancestral 'tasters' that have established which foods kill, which foods heal and which safely satiate hunger. In addition, we learn throughout our lives which foods agree with us and which don't. We also adopt and develop negative bias towards certain foods based around cultural taboos.

Generally, reactions of disgust are more likely to be linked to animal-based foods than plant-based ones and thus it is no surprise that the list of forbidden foods tends to revolve around those that are flesh based. Most religions have foods that are forbidden as they do not comply with that religion's purity code. Hindus do not eat beef, and many Buddhist teachings forbid the eating of all flesh; pork is off limits for Muslims while pig flesh and shellfish are out of bounds for Jews. The Christian Bible also lends teachings on 'clean' and 'unclean' food:

> The Lord said to Moses and Aaron, "Say to the Israelites: 'Of all the animals that live on land, these are the ones you may eat: You may eat any animal that has a divided hoof and that chews the cud.
>
> There are some that only chew the cud or only have a divided hoof, but you must not eat them. The camel, though it chews the cud, does not have a divided hoof; it is ceremonially unclean for you. The hyrax, though it chews the cud, does not have a divided hoof; it is unclean for you. The rabbit, though it chews the cud, does not have a divided hoof; it is unclean for you. And the pig, though it has a divided hoof, does not chew the cud; it is unclean for you. You must not eat their meat or touch their carcasses; they are unclean for you.
>
> Of all the creatures living in the water of the seas and the streams you may eat any that have fins and scales. But all creatures in the seas or streams that do not have fins and scales – whether among all the swarming things or among all the other living creatures in the water – you are to regard as unclean. And since you are to regard them as unclean, you must not eat their meat; you must regard their carcasses as unclean. Anything living in the water that does not have fins and scales is to be regarded as unclean by you.
>
> These are the birds you are to regard as unclean and not eat because they are unclean: the eagle,[a] the vulture,

the black vulture, the red kite, any kind of black kite, any kind of raven, the horned owl, the screech owl, the gull, any kind of hawk, the little owl, the cormorant, the great owl, the white owl, the desert owl, the osprey, the stork, any kind of heron, the hoopoe and the bat.'"

Most winged insects except those that swarm and jump were also included and creatures including geckos, rats and weasels were also classified as unclean and the message was clear: 'every creature that moves along the ground is to be regarded as unclean; it is not to be eaten. You are not to eat any creature that moves along the ground, whether it moves on its belly or walks on all fours or on many feet; it is unclean. Do not defile yourselves by any of these creatures. Do not make yourselves unclean by means of them or be made unclean by them.'

(Old Testament, Leviticus 11:47)

In addition, God told Noah not to drink the blood of any animal (Genesis 9:4), and Exodus 34:26 bans boiling a kid goat in its mother's milk. However, most Christians today overlook the advice in the Old Testament and enjoy their feasts of oysters, black pudding and bacon sarnies, defining 'unclean' meats as things that evoke their revulsion.

Disgust, then, is a highly cultural concept. Certain organic products such as rotting meat or fish are disgusting by nature, but many societies express somewhat idiosyncratic forms of disgust, which often have no basis beyond the development of rules and habits in their culture. In western societies, foods such as snails, frogs and offal may be exalted or considered repellent depending on geographical region and social group. This means that what we eat or repudiate speaks of far more than simple culinary preferences.

Two Bills of Fare, printed for John Weeks of the Bush-Tavern, Bristol, for Christmas 1790 and Christmas 1800 reveal fascinating and extensive menus, that list well over 100 dishes each of mostly fish, fowl and cuts of meat. The consideration of religious teachings certainly played second fiddle to that of culinary fashion and extravagance when it came to these menus. The 1790 bill of fare includes a roasting pig, reindeer tongue and a forty-seven pound turtle; whilst the 1800 menu includes a turtle weighing a hundred and twenty pounds. Numerous birds are listed including cuckoo, owls, golden plovers, swan, larks, sea pheasants (pintail duck) and stares (starlings). It certainly doesn't represent daily dining at this time, but it is worth noting that Georgian Britain did have a taste for the exotic, but of course to have such tastes you had to be affluent.

Turtle feasts became a kind of mania among the affluent classes and fashionable dinner parties were nothing without copious servings of freshly prepared turtle. Mock turtle made from calf's head became popular for those who could not afford the real thing frequently, but still wished to be a follower of culinary fashion. The taste for turtle, seems to lie within the fact that they were a rarity and expensive to procure caught in the West Indies, they had to be kept alive during the long voyage across the Atlantic before being slaughtered in Britain-many would not survive the voyage. Turtle warehouses sprang up in Bristol, where the turtle boats usually docked and so it is not a surprise to see turtles appearing on this menu.

Equally, those on the highest social rungs revelled in the delights of anything different and so unlike today, wild birds were seen as a delicacy and usually cooked in lard. Cuckoos like all birds would be enjoyed as a rare treat, alongside a variety of songbirds as and when they could be caught.

Animal tongues of all descriptions were a regular delicacy. Generally, either boiled or roasted, ox tongue was once a popular dish on the Christmas table. Reindeer tongue along with deer tongue were popular and would form a centre piece whole on a table or be sliced and served cold (just like other cold meats) or even chopped and included in things such as pies including the original mince pie. which included beef tongue, mutton or other meats.

Throughout history exotic meats and curious dishes went somewhere towards satisfying the appetite of a nation in which food was linked to status and entertainment and for which there was a thirst for more extravagant statements on the dinner table.

Every culture, in its own way, tends to divide what can be eaten from what cannot be eaten. Today, when we consider animal welfare, health concerns, environmental concerns, antibiotics in farming and the issue of intensively farmed animals, some people might consider becoming flexitarian, vegetarian or vegan, while for others the prospect of giving up meat, or of eating insects or lab-grown meat, provokes widespread scepticism, hostility and outright disgust. It is true to say that some people may pull a disgruntled face at the thought of a crunchy critter sandwich and baulk at the hypothesis that we'll all be eating insects in fifty years' time, but it is worth considering that not so long ago the prospect of eating frozen lamb from the other side of the world provoked a similar range of reactions in Victorian Britain. Imported frozen food and tinned products were all once new concepts that were treated with great mistrust and yet they are now commonplace. Furthermore, it must be considered that entomophagy (the eating of insects) is a common practice in many cultures, with beetles, caterpillars, bees, wasps and ants eaten as a standard menu item in much the same way that we might consider pie and chips mundane.

What we consider revolting is by no means set in stone and can also change over time, similarly how we classify the status of foods. Consider how the social standing of a lobster has changed from a poor man's food to a dish for the wealthy to relish with champagne.

The definition of revolting food, it seems, is an ever-changing one. What is imagined as revolting is highly dependent upon the cultural upbringing and the period in history to which the diner belongs.

Chapter 1

Death in a Tin

The story of the tin can is one of necessity, ingenuity and endurance, and one that affects every one of us. It has changed the way we eat, the way we shop, the way we manage our households and the way we travel. But its pioneers had humble ambitions – they just wanted to find a way of reliably preserving food and to solve the conundrum of how to feed troops and naval fleets while far away from a country's food supplies.

The invention of canning may have been heralded as a food preservation hero, but its path to success was a troubled one that was littered with scandal, putrefaction and even death.

Preserving food has been a preoccupation of mankind since the dawn of time; with preserving methods being an important undertaking for ensuring that there was a supply of food throughout the winter or in times of fresh food shortages, as well as for keeping seasonal harvests from going to waste. Early food preservation techniques were developed through necessity; it was a case of preserve or perish. Early preservation techniques were a combination of hypothesis, experiment and trial and error, and were perfected over time and through experience. These techniques including cooling, freezing, boiling, drying, curing, salting, smoking and pickling, and all have stood the test of time, proving so effective that they are still practised today.

Preserving food in the early modern period was still a task performed out of necessity. It was a duty that had great importance attached to it and it was the early modern housewife who shouldered the main responsibility for maintaining a well-stocked store cupboard and ensuring that ample food was stored unspoilt. In Gervase

Markham's domestic manual, *The English Huswife* (1615), the virtues of a 'compleate woman' are made very clear and it most evident that preservation skills are key: 'skill in [...] banqueting-stuffe, ordering of great feasts, preserving of all sorts of wines [...] distillations [...] the knowledge of dayries, office of malting, oats, their excellent uses in a family, brewing, baking, and all other things belonging to an houshold. (Markham, 1615).

To be a proficient housewife was to be skilled in preserving techniques and to assimilate the relevant domestic knowledge required for successful food preservation.

When examining illustrations and descriptions of Georgian larders the preservation techniques employed are ones that have a long ancestry and would not have been out of place in a Medieval larder. In fact, the techniques employed for food preservation remained very fixed until the innovations of the Victorian period.

Food imports up until the nineteenth century had always been limited to foods that were easy to transport without risk of spoiling and were thus confined to mainly spices, dried goods and those that would not go rancid or putrid during shipping. However, a Parisian confectioner, Nicholas Appert, was about to change the history of preserving and with it the world of food imports and export was set to change.

*****

It was undoubtedly Appert who laid the foundations of our modern canning process, though the stout glass bottles that Appert used to preserve his food in may at first glance seem unrelated.

From around 1790 onwards Appert began to research and trial food preservation techniques. Guarding against food spoilage was a priority at this time as natural resources were in short supply due to the outbreak of war and raw foods were spoiled during long military expeditions and manoeuvres. Developing a reliable way to preserve harvests was a good means of increasing food availability. Appert was aware of the flaws in the methods used for preserving:

> all the methods used up to now are restricted to two principles. One of them is based on desiccation, the other one appeals to an exogenous substance, added invariable amounts, to prevent putrefaction or fermentation processes from taking place. Desiccation destroys aroma, modifies the flavour, and hardens the fibre tissues. Sugar partially masks the taste which is supposed to be preserved. Salt gives an unpleasant acridity, hardens the animal substances which become indigestible and contracts vegetable parenchyma. Then, when one soaks the product to remove the salt, only the fiber element remains; and besides, they are spoiled. Vinegar can only be used to preserve a few products used as condiments.

Using these observations as the founding for his work, Appert took a very practical approach to the task of developing a reliable preservation method that was based on undeniable facts: 'the action of the fire destroys, or at least neutralizes, all the ferment which, in the nature, modify and deteriorate animals and plant material.' (Appert, p. 267)

Appert's method of preserving was inspired by wine making and involved packing fresh food into bottles and then immersing them in boiling water for several hours. He had to exclude all air and hold the jar tightly closed with cork, wire and sealing wax for this to be effective.

Appert was not familiar with the food science behind his method. Initially believing that it was the presence of air that led to spoilage, as is the case in wine production, many of his early experiments were focused on removing the air. His later experiments, however, led to him the conclusion that success was also due to subjecting his bottles to heat, though again without him understanding microbial spoilage.

The four stages of his process are clearly described by him:

1. *a renfermer dans les bouteilles ou bocaux les substances que l'on veut conserver.*
2. *A boucher ces diffèrents vases avec la plus grande attention; car, c'est principalement de 'l'opèration du bouchage que dèpend le succès.*
3. *A soumettre ces substances ainsi renfermèes, àl'action de l'eau bouillante d'un baine-marie, pendant plus ou moins de temps, selon leur nature et de la menière que je l'ibdiquerai pour chaque espèce de comestible;*
4. *A retirer les bouteilles du bain-marie au temps prescrit.*

After prolonged years of experimentation, Appert was ready to demonstrate to French government officials and authorities that his method could preserve fresh food without putrefaction in a portable form, making it suitable for use on army and navy expeditions. In 1803 the navy evaluated samples of three-month-old food preserved by Appert. The verdict was very positive: 'the meat broth is really good […] the boiled meat is eatable, yellow peas and garden peas possess the freshness and the flavour of recently harvested vegetables.' (Letter of the Conseil de Santé to General Caffarelli, préfet maritime, 1803)

The range of products that were preserved at Appert's factory in Massy were quite extensive and included everything from fruits and vegetables to eel and partridge. In a publicity stunt he even used his technique to preserve a whole sheep.

Catalogue of canned food products manufactured by Appert's workshops at Massy, France (Appert)

Basic Products
- Sorrel, asparagus, asparagus tip, fine garden peas, mean garden peas, wax bean, kidney beans, artichoke in quarters, whole artichoke, cauliflower,

chicory, spinach, tomato sauce, white currant, red currant, raspberry, cherry, morelle cherry, black currant, greengage, Mirabelle, nectarine, quince in quarters, apricot in quarters, peach in quarters, pear in quarters.

- Juice of: white currant, red currant, black currant, blackberry
- Must: sourish, deacidified or clarified
- Semi-condensed milk, whey, cream

Cooked Dishes
- Seasoned garden peas, seasoned rice
- Quenelle of carp, whiting
- Seasoned eel, seasoned pike, seasoned trout
- Undecut of young partridge, pheasant, woodcut, quail, teal, poulard, turkey, duck
- Croquette of turkey, young rabbit
- Various meats: lamb chop, chicken fricassee, mutton tongue, stewed lamp, pork pettitoes, pork undercut, cushion of veal, meat in jelly, stewing steak, beef steak, meat consommé, meat broth, egg in bechamelle sauce

Eager for recognition, in 1806 Appert went on to present a selection of bottled fruits and vegetables from his manufacture at the L'Exposition des Produits de l'Industrie Nationale in Paris. And though he did not receive any reward at the exhibition, he remained driven by his passion for preserving.

Appert was still looking for official recognition for his preserved foods, and in 1809 wrote to an institute devoted to the development of industrialisation in France (SEIN), where the most esteemed scientists of the epoch had a seat. Antoine Parmentier, first apothecary of Napoleon's armies, Louis-Bernard Guyton de Morveau and Amédée Buriat were chosen to examine Appert's research and results. His products were tasted and assessed by the members of the commission and their critique was mainly positive: 'the meat is soft, its taste is pleasant, the meat broth taste as good as a freshly prepared one, the milk is more yellow, more tasty and sweeter because it was condensed, same thing for the whey, garden peas are very good, cherries and apricots almost keep their savour, raspberry and redcurrant syrups keep their properties.' (Martin, 1807)

Appert proposed his development to the Ministre de l'Intérieur (Home Secretary) in 1809 as a solution to the predicament the army and navy faced in keeping food. The minister offered him two packages: he could patent the process and receive the royalties; or he could publish his preserving process. If he chose the latter option he would receive a considerable contribution of 12,000 French francs from the government. Appert chose the second proposal and accepted what was at the time a substantial financial award.

In 1810 he duly published details of his process including details of all the useful data and tips (Appert). Appert's book was a great success, enjoying fame and several print runs, being widely distributed and translated into German and English. He also received much praise from naval officers. Following its release many newspapers covered the story of the new food preservation technique: *Le Journal de l'Empire* (22 June 1810); *Le Journal du Commerce* (22 May 1810); *La Gazette de Santé* (22 July 1810). In the newspaper *Le Journalde Paris* (21 May 1810) the Ministre de l'Intérieur, le comte de Montalivet, described the significant advantages brought by the invention: 'travellers will be able to go from one hemisphere to the other one carrying an excellent meat broth, fresh milk [...] seaman won't be afraid anymore of scorbut.' While *Le Moniteur* of 1 September 1810 wrote: 'No one before had the talent to succeed in the food preserving. We are unanimously grateful to the most capable of the philanthropists.' (Barbier, 1994, p.208).

After the destruction of his manufacturing facility in 1814-15 by foreign troops, Appert received a silver medal from the SEIN.

He expected financial help but sadly this would not be forthcoming until 1824. In 1827 the SEIN awarded him a gold medal after an appreciatory report: 'this eminent manufacturer did the nation and the whole world a precious turn. His process was a great help for the sea service as they could have good and safe food. These products replaced salted provisions which were unhealthy and responsible for scurvy.' However, despite this accolade it is questionable whether the true scale and deep significance of Appert's work in preserving was recognised in his lifetime.

Appert's preserving process was of great help for the navy, allowing crews to enjoy wholesome and safe food, but it was also set to impact on world trade. It would in time determine what foods could be imported, how goods would be preserved and sold and what foods would be available both in the home pantry and at the warfront. It would also change the role of the housewife and the nature of preserving fresh produce. According to Parmentier and others, Appert was not the inventor of the process of preserving foodstuffs – housekeepers were doing this already – but his undeniable skill was in cultivating the process to develop a precise, detailed and reliable method of doing it on a large scale for manufacturing. (Parmentier, 1810). He is, therefore, considered to be the founding father of food canning.

*****

Appert's method had not only improved the diet of seamen but was also the seed that grew into a more reliable way of preserving food which would change how the average family ate. It is hard, therefore, to comprehend how the invention of the tin can was nearly an unsavory flop surrounded in scandal.

As Appert's method was so simple and already in the public domain, it was quickly adopted and those with good business sense saw a commercial opportunity. Augustus de Heine patented the use of iron and tin containers in February 1810, but never went into canning food on a commercial scale. Later that same year, Peter Durand, a British inventor and merchant, patented his own method using a tin can. The patent described a method of preserving animal food, vegetable food and other perishable articles using various vessels made of glass, pottery, tin or other suitable metals.

Durand experimented with larger quantities of food and was able to preserve over 13kg of meat in a single can. To give his method more of a footing and garner more authority for it, he asked the Royal Navy to take his cans on long trips that would last months at a time. Upon returning to shore, the contents were inspected by a few members of the Royal Society, and much to Durand's delight, the food was confirmed to be perfectly preserved.

However, like Augustus de Heine, Durand chose not to pursue the commercial production of tinned foods, and instead English businessmen Bryan Donkin and John Hall picked up the can and set about creating commercial-scale tinned food production.

How exactly Hall and Donkin got into the tinned food business is somewhat hazy. John Hall was the founder of of Dartford Iron Works and in the history of J. & E. Hall Ltd it is stated that John Hall and his associates paid £1,000 for 'a French Patent by a Chemist named Appert'. (Everard, 1935). Appert had no such patent to sell and the records of the firm Chevallier-Appert do not record any such transaction (International Tin Research & Development Council, 1939). Some versions of events tell of Hall and Donkin purchasing the patent from Durand, but whatever the facts, it is certain that Donkin and Hall saw the opportunity for making a flourishing business out of food preserved in robust iron vessels.

The course of true invention, like love, doesn't always run smoothly and a few years were spent in the development stage before Donkin and Hall's new factory in Blue Anchor Road, Bermondsey, was in a position to send out samples for suitability trials for use in the army and navy. However, once the teething problems were over and the samples were dispatched, correspondence shows that there was strong praise and support for the tinned foods.

In a letter dated 30 April 1813 from Culling Charles Smith on behalf of Lord Wellesley (later Duke of Wellington), it is noted that his Lordship had found Donkin's preserved beef very good. (International Tin Research & Development Council, 1939). In 1814 Sir Joseph Banks, then President of the Royal Society, wrote to give his consent to his name 'being placed among the very respectable names which are printed in your Prospectus, as giving their testimony in favour of the nutritious qualities of your embalmed provisions.' On 15 July 1815 Sir Joseph wrote again to explain that the fillet of veal which had been canned in December 1812, and which he had taken receipt of in January 1813, had been opened and successfully devoured. He wrote that contents of the tin were 'declared by the unanimous vote of the party present [...] to be in a perfect state of preservation and had not lost any of its nutritious qualities.' Indeed, the praise and testimonials for the tinned goods were abundant and were showcased in the company's 1817 brochure.

The process of can making was a ground-breaking one in the world of food preservation, but also a labour-intensive one, with sheets of tin plate being transformed by hand into cans filled with preserved food that was destined for every corner of the British Empire.

The early cans ranged from 4lb to 20lb in weight and they contained things such as concentrated soup, seasoned mutton, boiled mutton, roasted veal, veal and vegetables, boiled beef, corned round of beef and vegetable soup. The concept may have been novel, but there was great innovation not just in the way food was preserved but also in terms of quality assurance. Each can made at the factory spent one month of incubation at 90-110°C before leaving and each was numbered to help track and trace its origins – a well-known food safety system today but one that was pioneering at the time.

The endorsement of tinned food products continued to flow freely. In 1813 the Admiralty bought 156lb of Donkin's food, feeding it to ailing sailors, because it was mistakenly thought that scurvy was due to an over-reliance on salted meat.

William Warner, surgeon of the ship *Ville de Paris*, wrote in 1814 that tinned food 'forms a most excellent restorative to convalescents, and would often, on long voyages, save the lives of many men who run into consumption at sea for want of nourishment after acute diseases; my opinion, therefore, is that its adoption generally at sea would be a most desirable and laudable act.'

With high commendations in ready supply, business with the Admiralty took off and by 1818 Messrs Donkin, Hall and Gamble were supplying substantial amounts of their preserved foods to the navy, giving rise to further positive reviews and medical testimonies.

In 1818 some of Donkin's tinned provisions were taken on the expedition in *HMS Isabella* and *Alexander* to Baffin's Bay. The commander, John Ross, noted in his diary on 8 September 1818 that once fresh provisions were spent, orders were given for serving a proportion of preserved foods in lieu of part of the salted meats provisions.

On 9 December 1820 (sgd.) C.I. Bevereley wrote, 'I have no hesitation in pronouncing my opinion that to judicious employment of these articles is to be attributed in great measure, the preservation of the general health of the Officers and Crew of *H.M. Brig Griper*, and to the same means is to be ascribed the recovery of the individual attached by the scurvy.'

Despite such proven success, Donkin's interest in tinned goods ended in 1821 when he dissolved his partnership with Hall and Gamble. It is not clear why, but the impression from his diaries is that canning was more of an engineering challenge than a passion for food preservation.

As Donkin stepped down, his successor at the helm of the world's first tin canning business, John Gamble, moved the factory to Cork in Ireland in 1830, where there was a larger supply of cattle and the shipping route to the United States of America offered a steady supply of custom.

In 1841 an important patent was filed by Stephan Goldner. British Patent No. 8873 was to signal a competitor in the world of canning. Goldner's patent cited that of John Wertheimer's (patent No. 8874) and used the same address as Wertheimer's. Both parties registered the idea of canned food preservation using calcium chloride instead of water. This was heralded as being even safer than the 'traditional' water bath method because the calcium chloride allowed for higher temperatures to be reached and thus reduced the risk of incomplete sterilisation and putrefaction of the contents.

Goldner was fast in securing a contract to supply the Admiralty. In 1845 he obtained a substantial order for tinned food for Franklin's expedition in *HMS Erebus* and *HMS Terror*. The order was for approximately 22,000 pints of soup, 5,500lb of vegetables and 31,000lb of meat. Ships for such expeditions carried three years of preserved foods so the volume can well be imagined. The rushed contract was given to Goldner on 1 April 1845, a mere seven weeks before Franklin's ill-fated expedition was due to set sail, and it is evident that Goldner was experiencing some difficulty in fulfilling the order in such a short timeframe. On 5 May 1845 the superintendent at the victualling yard in Deptford reported to his board that only one tenth of the order had been supplied and on the 8 May Goldner promised that the remaining order would be supplied as follows: all the meat by 12 May, and soups by the 15 May. However, this assertion was made with the condition that he be allowed to supply the soups in canisters larger than specified. The board granted his request and agreed the revised delivery dates.

When Goldner asked in November 1845 if it were possible to find out if there were any reports on the preserved meat and how it had been received, he was told that this was not possible. It is inconceivable that Goldner could have ever imagined how badly the meat was actually doing and that no less than 15,420lb would be condemned as unfit for consumption. The fate of Goldner's consignment and that of Franklin's expedition would not become apparent for several years. Tinned foods continued to soar in popularity and Goldner's business continued to grow.

When Gamble exhibited an array of canned foods at the Great Exhibition in 1851 to widespread approval it must have seemed like they were on the brink of becoming a household must-have as well as a means of supplying military rations. However, the fate of canning as a food preservation method was soon to hang in the balance with the revelation of a food scandal that would threaten to kill the fledgling industry.

*****

In January 1852 a group of meat inspectors gathered at the Royal Clarence Victualling Yard in Portsmouth and proceeded to open 306 cans of meat destined for the navy.

It was not until they opened the nineteenth can that they discovered any contents that were fit for human consumption. Instead of preserved beef, they found putrid meat that was in such advanced stages of decomposition that the stone floors needed to be coated with chloride of lime to mask the stench, according to an account in the *Illustrated London News*.

The smell was so unwholesome and overpowering that at times the inspectors had to stop and leave the room for fresh air. During the course of their investigations they fished out pieces of heart, rotting tongues from a dog or sheep, offal, blood, a whole kidney 'perfectly putrid', ligaments and tendons and a mass of pulp. Some organs appeared to be from diseased animals.

They condemned 264 cans that day, throwing them into the sea. The remaining forty-two cans that were deemed acceptable were given to the poor.

This scene was repeated across the country, as part of a nationwide inspection ordered by the Admiralty. A letter to *The Times* in 1853 revealed that officers of *The Plover* threw 1,570lb of canned meat overboard in the Bering Straits because 'we found it in a pulpy, decayed and putrid state, and totally unfit for men's food'.

Stephan Goldner was the supplier of this decaying mess in tins and it unfolded that he had been able to win the Admiralty contract by undercutting all rivals, engaging cheap labour at his meat factory in what is now Romania.

The average weight of a Donkin, Hall and Gamble's meat tin was 6lb whereas Goldners tins held between 9lb and 14lb of meat. It would eventually be reported that Goldner's tins were simply too large; the bacteria in the centre of the tin being able to survive the heat treatment because of its large volume and breed after sealing. The fact that it was the larger tins that frequently spoiled supports this theory.

Goldner had won his contract in 1845 and supply had increased when the Admiralty introduced preserved meat as a general ration one day a week in 1847. However, the following year complaints began to filter in from victualling yards in the UK and from British seamen around the world regarding quality and also reporting that undesirable parts of animals were being found in canned meat.

In 1847 concern about Franklin's disappearance began to be expressed by the Admiralty in London. In 1850 twelve search expeditions were mounted to find evidence of what happened to the well-provisioned expedition. One search team found something of interest on Beechey Island. There they found wooden shelters and three graves with tombstones indicating that two seamen had died in January and one in April of 1846. Also found nearby was a discarded pile of 700 tins of Goldner's consignment, some still full, along with other supplies from the Franklin expedition (Cookman, 2000).

In March 1854 the Admiralty declared, 'the officers and ship's company are to be removed from the Navy List and are to be considered as having died in service. Wages are to be paid to their relatives to that date.' The Franklin expedition was resigned at this point to a tragic and mysterious loss. However, in October of that year Dr John Rae would make discoveries that shed more light on fate of the crew of the failed mission.

Rae had lived for sixteen years in the northern reaches of Canada as an officer in the Hudson Bay Company, and was exploring the Boothia Peninsula when he encountered a story from the local Inuit people. Dr Rae was familiar with the Inuit survival techniques in the Arctic (McCoogan, 2001) and it was this knowledge that allowed him to learn important information about the fate of Franklin's expedition. Little could John Rae have known that he would be castigated for telling the unpalatable truth – that sailors in the Royal Navy had resorted to cannibalism before perishing.

The Inuit told Rae of finding the bodies of thirty white men to the north, and suspecting that souvenirs would have been taken, he enquired and subsequently bartered for them, eventually acquiring naval clothing, monogrammed ship's cutlery and a kettle. The possessions were evidence that the crew had perished and Rae's report stated: 'Some of the bodies had been buried (probably those of the first victims of famine); some were in a tent or tents; others under the boat, which had been turned over to form a shelter, and several lay scattered about in different directions.' If his findings had ended there he would have been credited for his work, and Victorian society would no doubt have been content that a terrible tragedy had occurred and Rae had been the man to deliver the tragic news. But Rae had made a disturbing discovery when he happened upon the contents of the kettle: human remains. He recorded in his report: 'From the mutilated state of many of the bodies and the contents of the kettles, it is evident that our wretched Countrymen had been driven to the last dread alternative – cannibalism – as a means of prolonging existence.'

Such findings were too gruesome for Victorian society to stomach. Furthermore, Lady Jane Franklin wished to prevent her husband's good name from being tainted and set out to sully Rae's name and credibility. She elicited the support of novelist Charles Dickens who castigated the Orkney explorer in a letter to *The Times* for daring to suggest that British naval officers would 'resort to native practices'.

Rae's findings were simply too horrifying for the sentimental and patriotic Victorians to swallow. His publication of his macabre discoveries led to him being vilified in the newspapers. Charles Dickens described their testimony as 'the chatter of a gross handful of uncivilised people', and accused the 'lying savages' of murdering the sailors and concocting the cannibalism story to cover their own crime. No one wanted to believe that stalwart British citizens might resort to the heinous crime of eating each other.

Rae's character was assassinated and his professional integrity shattered. His report was dismissed as unreliable because it relied solely on the accounts of the Inuit. Rae did not actually visit the main burial site, saying that the Inuit were reluctant to make the ten- or twelve-day trek to the site of the lost expedition, and his 'failure' to visit the site led to considerable criticism.

In 1859 McClintock's search for traces of the Franklin expedition on the west coast of King William Island resulted in several major discoveries that included an official record containing the dates of Sir John Franklin's death, details of the abandonment of *HMS Erebus* and *HMS Terror*, and of the departure of the ship's company for the Back River.

Despite the evidence discovered by Rae and McClintock, Lady Franklin was still not convinced that all questions surrounding her husband's disappearance had been answered. In the 1860s, as support in Britain for further exploration waned, she found new support in the American journalist Charles Francis Hall and his patron Henry Grinnell, a wealthy New York businessman and philanthropist. Grinnell funded two expeditions by Hall in search of evidence from the Franklin expedition, the first to Baffin Island in 1860, when Hall engaged two Inuit natives, Ipirvik and Taqulittuq, to serve as his interpreters and guides. He staged his second, longer expedition in search of Franklin's party between 1864 and 1869 when he based himself initially at Repulse Bay (now Naujaat) in the Kivalliq region on the northwestern side of Hudson Bay. Hall's findings supported those of previous investigations and confirmed that the ill-fated expedition had ended in cannibalism.

Over the next two decades a skeleton with the limbs sawed off, a box of skulls in a lifeboat, and scattered relics were found by American explorer Frederick Schwatka and so the evidence of cannibalism became overwhelming. However, a real explanation of what caused the deaths of the initial twenty-four crewmen would not come until a century later.

In 1981 Owen Beattie, from the University of Alberta, established the Franklin Forensic Project and led two scientific expeditions to exhume the remains of the three sailors that had been left undisturbed by previous research expeditions. The remains of John Torrington, John Hartnell and William Braine were analysed and high lead levels were recorded in all three bodies. In Beattie's follow-up analysis he found the lead to be consistent isotopically to that from the tinned cans. (Kowal W, 1991).

In 1992 Anne Keenleyside studied more than 400 human bone parts on King William Island. When examined, the presence of knife marks on many of the remains was confirmed (Keenleyside, 1997). It was estimated that the bones were the remains of between eight and eleven expedition members and it was concluded that they had been dismembered and eaten, thus confirming Dr John Rae's earliest findings on the fate of Franklin's crew. However, it was well documented that the expedition was exceptionally well-stocked with provisions and so the question was whether the good quality provisions that Franklin boasted had actually turned out to have been inedible due to putrefaction and therefore forced the crew into cannibalism. Perhaps more importantly, could the tinned food that was consumed have been toxic?

When looking at the chemical evidence of lead poisoning and Beattie's findings it is necessary to look at the business practices of

Stephen Goldner, the manufacturer who undercut his competitors for the supply of tinned provisions to the Admiralty for many years. Several tins from the discarded pile found on Beechey Island were inspected by Beattie. The technology for preparing canned meat at that time was new, having only been patented in 1811, and the cans were sealed with a solder of tin and a high lead content. The soldering itself is now known to have contained a mixture of 90% lead and 10% tin. The tins themselves were also poorly made, with gaps in the soldering allowing air to permeate and the food inside to spoil.

It seems likely that in a bid to cut costs and fulfil the contract at such short notice corners had been cut which included poor quality canning, insufficient cooking and suspect hygiene practices. The poor-quality canning practices could have led to botulism before evidence of food spoilage was apparent to the naked eye.

Despite the growing number of complaints about the quality and safety of Goldner's tinned provisions in 1849 from HM Victualling Yards, Goldner was awarded further contracts with the strict understanding that meat needed to be genuine. However, the volume of complaints could no longer be overlooked. Horrific stories of putrid and unwholesome flesh being canned at the Romanian factory not only shed great suspicion upon the practices of Goldner's canning operation but also caused distrust of canning as a safe preservation technique.

Amidst the damaging reports of condemned consignments of Goldner's meat, a government select committee was appointed to investigate the problem. The committee reached the conclusion that the chief cause of canned meat spoiling was a failure to ensure the complete expulsion of air from the can and adequate cooking of the contents. A direct link to the larger size of the tins and purification was made. Goldner was banned from supplying the navy with tinned food and his pleas to be allowed another opportunity were ignored. In addition to the damning committee findings, it was also revealed that Goldner had supplied the meat to Sir John Franklin's ill-fated expedition. People were left to draw their own conclusions on the part played by Goldner's tinned goods in the fate of Franklin's crew, but needless to say that the public's trust of canning was shaken.

The unfavorable publicity in 1852 dampened the growing popularity of tinned goods among the public. However, the cattle plague in Britain in the 1860s instigated a steep rise in the price of fresh meat and stimulated the demand for cheaper alternatives – a need that tinned meat was able to fulfil. Tinned food was thrown a lifeline and its path to becoming a household staple was back on track.

In1865 the doctor and writer Andrew Wynter said: 'It does seem suicidal folly on the part of the public to conceive a prejudice against a discovery which is of great public importance in a hygienic point of view, and which has been attested and proved.' By the 1870s tinned meat was roughly half the price of fresh, so it is perhaps not surprising that by 1880 the UK was importing 16 million lb of canned meat as new industries developed around the globe, capitalising on a growing network of railways, roads and canals that were making logistics easier than ever before.

The earliest use of the word tinned to refer to food given by the Oxford English Dictionary is an 1861 reference by Mrs Beeton to 'tinned turtle' (Beeton, 1861). The market for tins was certainly an expanding one by the late Victorian period and in the 1895 edition of *Mrs Beeton's Book of Household Management* it states: 'an important trade has sprung up within the last quarter of a century in tinned foods of various kinds.' The accompanying illustration shows in excess of eighty products, including tinned fruit, lunch tongues, boiled mutton, and other products such as potted beef, 'extra choice rabbits' and 'fresh oysters'.

The Goldner scandal and tales of poor quality and dubious contents gave the more prosperous housewife cause to distrust tinned food. There was also a widely held belief that it was immoral to save labour, especially in the case of servants. Indeed, Mrs Beeton quotes the Bible on this matter, advising 'the mistress' that 'She looketh well to the ways of her household, and eateth not the bread of idleness.' (Beeton, *Mrs Beeton's Book of Household Management*, 1895).

Nevertheless, tinned food was becoming a popular addition to the larder and a staple of the British diet which Mrs. Beeton admitted 'Tinned Meats, Soups, Fish, Poultry, Fruit and Vegetables now occupy an important place in our food supply, being available at any time, and handy substitutes when fresh provisions may be difficult to procure.' (Beeton, Mrs Beeton's Book of Household Management, 1895)

Canned goods in late Victorian England were mostly imported, brought in from as far afield as Australasia, Argentina and the United States. During this period British manufacturing took a backseat in canning until after the Great War as the competition from overseas was so great. Indeed, from the mid-1860s vast quantities of canned mutton and beef were imported from Australia as it was far cheaper than any meat that could be produced in Britain, where livestock farmers were struggling to meet demand because of outbreaks of various animal diseases such as foot and mouth, bovine pleuro-pneumonia and rinderpest.

Some staples were prepared by British manufacturers, including the Army and Navy Stores who prepared dishes such as boiled mutton and steak and kidney pudding (Society, 1969), as well as calf's sweetbreads with truffles, whole roast grouse, pâtes de foie gras, and lobsters in aspic designed for the more distinguished palette.

As canned meat flowed into the British ports from the United States, Australia and Argentina and were proudly displayed in the shop windows of every grocers, it seemed that the dawn of 'convenience food' had arrived. Canned salmon from Columbia and Alaska was exported all over the world and in 1886 Fortnum and Masons purchased the entire stock of baked beans from H.J. Heinz, just in from America (though this novelty was slow to catch on with British households).

****

It seems that tinned food just couldn't keep out of the headlines, however, and in 1895 there was more scandal, this time about American tinned meat.

On 9 March 1895 *The Weekly News* covered a report in *The Times* on the unsanitary preparation of meat in US factories that was destined for England and other European countries.

> It is the custom there [in the United States] for inspectors to be placed in every slaughter-house in order to condemn any and every animal unfit for human food [...] Should an animal be suffering from "lumpy jaw" (actinomycosis), or any other evident disease, the inspector condemns it, and sees it killed, skinned, cut up, and carted to what is termed "the tank room", where it is supposed to go through a process of steaming, after which it becomes "fertilizer stock". The tongue, however, is apt to be overlooked, as also the fat taken from inside the diseased animal. The tongue is thrown with others, smoked, canned, and sent into the export trade. That fat is used as a source of "oleo", which goes towards making refined "oleo-margarine".
>
> In the tank room the diseased meat is, in the presence of the inspector, put into a clean tank, the lid of which is then screwed on, pre- paratory to turning in the steam by which the destruction is supposed to be completed. But directly the inspector has returned to the slaughterhouse, the lid is taken off, and, as rapidly as hands can do it, the condemned meat is lifted out, carted promptly to the chill rooms, and mixed with other stock awaiting purchasers [...] Speaking of a particular firm, our correspondent states that, for the sake of a few paltry dollars, "this firm will condemn thousands of human beings to chances of sickening and even dying from loathsome diseases contracted through eating some diseased meat."

He remarks, moreover, that this is a subject which must interest everyone, rich or poor, since so much American beef is consumed in England.

The worrying story of diseased meat and unscrupulous practices continued in the article as it described in graphic detail how extract of beef was prepared and how foreign bodies during processing were dealt with:

Certain circumstances incidental to the preparation of a so-called "extract of beef" are almost too revolting for publication. This concoction, "extract of filth" as our correspondent calls it, is offered to the public in dainty jars, but is [...] made of the refuse from the canning rooms and cellars, and is thus something very different from the luscious extract of "choice cuts of beef" which the consumer may innocently think he purchases.

The room in which this compound is prepared is described as containing at times a "typhoid atmosphere". "The smell," says our correspondent, "sickened me completely. The surroundings of the room were filthy. There were several cans lying around containing the extract in its crude state, and several trucks containing the liquid extract of beef. Whilst standing there, two fully-developed rats that had fallen into one of these cans of extract and had been drowned were pulled out by the man in charge of this department, just previous to using the contents. How long they had been there cannot be proved, but [...] decomposition had already set in and the skins and hair were leaving the body, and this is an everyday occurrence."

Just in case the thought of a decomposing rat floating around in a vat of extract of beef or diseased meat finding its way into tinned food wasn't enough to make the consumer wary, there were plenty of stories in the press of ill-fate befalling those who partook in a meal of tinned food.

Today, few things seem less exciting than a tin of salmon. It is the stuff that old aunts and grandmothers mashed with vinegar and served with cucumber in sandwiches, and it is hard to think of eating a tinned salmon sandwich as dicing with death. The newspapers of the late nineteenth and early twentieth century, however, were full of stories of ptomaine poisoning. The terror of the botulism bacteria and the chaos it could wreak was well canvassed and canned meats and fish became a source of suspicion and concern.

Headlines of poisoning and death frequently accompanied descriptions of unfortunate cases where consuming tinned food had led to illness or, in extreme cases, death. Three such headlines involved tinned lobster:

POISONED BY TINNED LOBSTER. A CASE FROM THE MUMBLES.
A holiday visitor to the Mumbles, a super- annuated inspector of the Metropolitan Police Force, has been a patient at the Swansea Hospital for a week owing to blood poisoning. The ex-inspector was seized with severe illness after having partaken of a, meal of tinned lobster, which, he says seemed to be good, for he ate and enjoyed it immensely.

South Wales Daily News
15 August 1899

POISONED BY TINNED LOBSTER
The other afternoon the Birmingham Coroner held an inquest respecting the death of Thomas Roberts Thomas, a solicitor's managing clerk. The deceased had for a very considerable time been in the habit of making a supper

once a week of tinned lobster, and on August 1, when purchasing the lobster, he was advised to have a particular kind on account of that asked for not being quite right later he became seriously ill, and died on Weane day from ptomaiue poisoning. A verdict of poisoning from eating tinned lobster was recorded.

The Cardigan Observer and General Advertiser for the
Counties of Cardigan Carmarthen and Pembroke
18 sept 1897

DEATH FROM EATING TINNED LOBSTER
At the village of Herne, near Canterbury, a boy, named Excell, has died from blood poisoning, which is supposed to have been caused by the eating of some tinned lobster, his illness having commenced the day after he had partaken of a meal from a newly-opened canister of that fish.

South Wales Echo (5th edition)
2 October 1886

Lobster was a popular and sought-after provision in the Victorian era and tinned lobster made for a convenient and cost effective way to enjoy this delicacy. We have a long history of eating lobsters in the Stone Age and it was a source of normal nourishment enjoyed as a regular food.

Indeed it wasn't until after the Viking era that the status of fish and shellfish began to change, partly because of the religious rules surrounding the consumption of meat and the stipulation of 'fysshe' only days increased demand for lobster and other seafoods. With an increased demand for flesh that was not forbidden, puffins, beavers' tails, barnacle geese and infant rabbits were all classified as fish whilst lobster climbed the social ladder and began to appear on the tables of the wealthy and influential; accounts for the Bishop of Salisbury from the 1400s record forty-two types of shellfish purchased in a nine-month period. Whilst in the fifteenth century boiling lobsters became popular as did the fashion for eating them cold with vinegar.

However, lobsters did present the worry of freshness as a fresh lobster would need to be cooked and eaten within two days, whereas a pre-boiled lobster offered convenience but a short shelf life. Wealthy Britons enjoyed potted lobster and entertained with rich lobster sauces as recipes for fricassèeing, stewing and simmering lobsters in creamy sauces or wine appeared in fashionable recipe books. Charles Dickens' wife included a recipe for fish served with lobster sauce in one of her menus for a grand dinner in 1852. In her cookbook *What shall we have for dinner?,* written under her pseudonym Lady Maria Clutterbuck, she celebrated lobster as a rising star in high society dining. Lobster was rising in popularity and canned lobster was something Donkin-Hall were primed to produce. With advances in ice production, travel networks and food preservation in the form of canning, lobster consumption increased and tinned lobster was a convenient addition to sauces and prepared dishes as well as a welcome supper treat for the discerning palate of modest means.

As the journalist George Dodd noted in his 1856 volume *The Food of London*: 'Lobsters [...] are more influenced by recent improvements in rapid conveyance than most other fish.' According to Dodd, London consumed 1.5 million lobsters worth a total of £30,000 each year. The perishability of fresh lobster had long been a concern, but tinned lobster seemed to avoid this problem. However, being a highly desirable commodity, traders were at pains to limit the number of tins that were damaged or past their best, meaning that devious practices such as re-soldering blown cans occurred. In the 1897 case of Clara Green, who died from eating tinned lobster aged thitry-four, 'The tin [of lobster] was [...] examined by the coroner and jury, and two holes were found to have been soldered from the outside.' In her case 'The jury returned a verdict of Death from ptomaine poisoning, caused by eating tinned lobster.' (Poisoned by Tinned Lobster, 1897).

Warnings about the dangers of consuming damaged tins circulated and so great was the concern over death through tinned food that, in 1897, the Medical Officer of Health of St. Pancras advised that 'many cases of poisoning from eating canned delicacies are due to the fact that so much of the tinned foods in the, cheaper markets is derived from old ships' stores.' (Dangers of Tinned Food, 1897). He called for date stamping of each can to alert the consumer to the age of the tins they were looking to consume. The idea of date stamping the tins was not seen as a solution to tinned food safety, with the *Daily Graphic* stating, 'the notion is a good one, but it is doubtful whether it would be entirely effectual.'

Leaflets were circulated regarding tinned food safety and advice on avoiding damaged tins was published, but despite advice the newspapers continued to be filled with details of deaths caused by the consuming of tinned food.

Most canned food spoilage is fairly obvious upon visual inspection: either the can itself becomes deformed or its contents are visibly spoiled. In most cases spoilage is undesirable, but relatively harmless, perhaps leading to digestive upset or a mild illness, but headlines proclaiming death by tinned food continued to be emblazoned on newstands.

The headlines of ptomaine poisoning must be looked at in an historical context. Today we would understand that ptomaines are the by-products of bacterial decomposition of animal and vegetable protein. They do not cause food poisoning, but were previously thought to. Indeed in a 1915 book entitled *Food and Feeding in Health and Disease* (Watson, 1915) it is explained that ptomaine poisoning can 'arise from tainted meat, milk, or fish, more especially shellfish. Ptomaines are alkaloidal substances produced by decomposition, or putrefaction of proteins under the influence of bacterial action.' Ptomaine poisoning remained a vague and general term used for food poisoning regardless of its origin.

Today it is likely that we would have attributed death from eating tinned food as being the result of *Clostridium botulinum*.

This bacterium produces botulinum, the deadliest toxin known to humankind, which can't be detected by sight, smell, or taste. Botulism doesn't itself cause tins to be externally deformed, but those external signs often suggest a poor quality canning process, which can breed both botulism and other kinds of bacteria that have more visible effects. Botulism is also anaerobic, meaning it thrives in oxygen-free environments, such as those offered in canned food.

Tinned salmon and lobster were particularly prone to botulism if not heated and processed properly and carefully during canning. There is only so much heat that the tinned salmon will stand before it becomes unpalatable and this is apparently very near to the temperature required to kill the bacteria so any that was even slightly underdone would be a potential risk.

Though most of the unsavoury tales regarding tinned food involved tinned meat or fish, there were quite a few scandals involving tinned fruit. A newspaper report from 31 March 1900 tells of how forty guests at a hotel were struck by food poisoning and two of them died. The alleged cause of the poisoning was tinned fruit cocktail. Entitled 'ptomaine Poisoning. Caution To Hotel Keepers', the article describes how 'poisoning was brought about by the generation of bacteria, probably in some tinned food. The hotel chef admitted in evidence that when using tinned fruit he left what remained in the tin until next day, and then used it.' The plaintiffs were awarded £140 compensation, but this would not have assisted the two unfortunate souls who were served a bowl of deadly fruit cocktail.

It seems that there were several issues at play in the safety of tinned goods. The first was the quality of the food being tinned. Then there was the sanitation and honesty of the canning factory: the matter of due diligence in the preparation and execution of the tins including heating and sealing the tins efficiently. Then there was the issue of rogue traders who sought to peddle unsound tins of food and in some cases befuddle their customers by disguising the state of their unsound goods and thus swindling them into purchasing tins unfit for consumption.

Reports of unscrupulous trading and tinned food being seized as unfit for human consumption were splashed across the weekly rags and served as a warning to the penny-wise housewife looking to make economies in the purchase of groceries. In 1897 such a tale of an unsound tinned food was told in vivid colour:

> A vigorous crusade is being carried on against vendors of unsound tinned foods by the Sanitary Authorities of the Vestry of St. Matthew, Bethnal Green. A number of SEIZURES have been made and prosecutions started, but so widespread is the practice of selling "blown" tinned fish, milk, and fruit that it has become necessary to issue a circular of warning to the residents of the parish […] for the guidance of the public it is pointed out that the vendor of old and unfit foods known as "job lines" endeavors to evade detection by piercing the tins and so liberating the accumulated gases, and then resolders and relabels the tins. In one shop in Aldgate the *Daily Mail* representative saw roughly 100 tins of lobster that had been pierced and resoldered, in some cases two or three times.
>
> (Unsound Tinned Food, 1900)

Another headline from 1899 read 'Seizure Of Tinned Food' before going on to explain that Joseph and Vernon Fells had been summonsed to answer charges for the 'possession of a quantity of tinned food unfit for the food of man. It was stated that in one box containing 72 tins of Honey brand condensed milk no less than 59 were blown. Fresh labels had been put on many of the tins. Out of 39 tins of "Finest Columbia" salmon 10 were bad, and from a package of 336 tins of condensed milk no less than 231 were bad. There were also 501 tins of bad sardines, and 72 tins of pine-apples were in a like condition. In a shed were 792 tins of condensed milk, all bad."

Given the scandals of putrid meat and reports of unsafe tinned goods it is surprising that there continued to be any demand for tinned food, yet tinned goods managed to secure themselves a place in British pantries due to their cost and convenience. Even after the 1970's tinned salmon botulism scare when 'Britons were warned [...] against eating any canned salmon from the United States or Canada following four cases of food poisoning' (*New York Times*, 1978), tinned food sales continued to rise.

Not even the modern love affair with fresh food has managed to kill off our beloved tinned provisions. It is certain that things such as tinned fruits and meats are not as popular today as they were fifty years ago and stores like Fortnum and Masons, which were once instrumental in trailblazing this grand experiment, now only stock tinned foie gras. Tinned food appears to be here to stay, although its presence may be limited. It has proven itself capable of riding bad publicity storms throughout history, but it seems its fate is to languish in the back of a cupboard waiting for an emergency when it might be considered a last resort. Tinned meals now represent a far less appetising prospect than fresh or chilled prepared versions.

Chapter 2

The Offal Truth

'Till cramm'd and gorg'd, nigh burst with suckt and glutted offal.'

Milton, *Paradise Lost*, X. 633

When it comes to eating animal innards it seems that it excites extreme reactions, both positive and negative. Whilst some people will recount with relish their memories of a succulent supper of pig's trotters others will recoil in horror at the mere suggestion of a kidney in a steak pie.

The history of eating offal is a long and changing one. Once a cheap and wholesome source of food that was prized for its nutritional qualities and heartiness, offal was at the centre of many regional specialities and championed in home economy. Increasingly, though, offal has come to be seen as being all the bits we don't wish to talk or think about, let alone eat. It seem that our sensibilities are insulted by the thought of essential organs: glands, skin, muscle, guts, gizzards, hearts, kidneys, lungs, marrow, spleens, tongues, trotters and testicles are often considered too much to stomach. Head cheese and brain fritters have fallen from the grace of most dining rooms, and along with dishes of steaming hot tripe and cowheel jelly they are now considered revolting, although offal is not completely off the menu. In addition to those who love a bit of liver fried in butter and see a pork chop with a kidney attached as a delicacy, there are the fanatical nose-to-tail eaters and celebrity chefs who have been keen to extol the virtues of eating the gory bits as well as prime cuts. Then there are the many fashionable restaurants that have started to feature offal on the menu. It seems that if it is expensive and fashionable enough then consumers are willing to set aside their strong aversions and try specialities such as sweetbreads, tripe and ox cheek. Even those who cower in fear at the very thought of bloody entrails will themselves eat offal, albeit without full cognisance, in basic staples such as sausages, hotdogs, pies and burgers.

There is no doubt that offal incorporates all the less prized pieces of meat that can truly put a cook's ability to the test: kidneys, liver, sweetbreads, chicken giblets, lamb intestines, cow's udder and pigs' feet are not ingredients that can be carelessly slopped in a microwave and left to cook, nor for that matter will they take kindly to being cooked without care in an oven or in a frying pan, but it is surely not these reason that cause looks of horror and stomach-churning reactions. Perhaps it is the fact that things like hearts, livers, and kidneys are the life force of an animal and are so instantly recognisable and comparative to our own organs serving as a reminder of mortality that we find disconcerting. Is it the fact that some offal resembles actual animal 'parts' which is just too much for our modern culture that is so often divorced from butchering? In the era of the chicken 'nugget' and turkey 'dinosaur' an actual tongue, heart, tail or ear tends to remind the eater that the food is not from some anonymous cut of 'meat' but is actually from an animal that once lived and breathed before being slaughtered and butchered for human food. Or is offal rejected because of the association of specific body parts – e.g., feet, snouts, tongues, genitals – with being dirty or undesirable? Whatever the reasons for rejection, the history of eating offal is far longer than our rejection of it. So when did we decide offal had become awful and does it deserve its revolting reputation?

It is certain that offal has historically enjoyed great culinary admiration, adorning the very best tables. At a feast for the knights of the fleece, in December 1545, there were dishes of beef and mutton, hams and tongues, soups, calves' heads, venison with turnips, mashed pease, veal, hot swan (*signe chault*), goose, hens, turkeys, pies of cows' udders and *entremets*. This rather copious feast of food was followed by roasted sausages, tripe cutlets, ragouts and pies of venison and partridges, roast pheasants, capons and pigeons. Once these delicacies had been sufficiently enjoyed the final serving included peacocks, partridges, water-hens, brawn, hot pigeon pies, cold heron pies, roasted rabbits and geese as well as jellies and other dishes. There was plenty of offal and dishes that we perhaps wouldn't imagine or even consider eating today. Whilst this feast was rather overwhelming by today's standards, simpler dishes such as 'umble' pie made good use of entrails. Though this dish is often portrayed as being a peasant recipe, it was also enjoyed by the wealthier classes.

The recipe featured in Robert May's *The Accomplisht Cook* of 1660 using nutmeg and claret:

> To make Umble Pies
> Lay minced beef-suet in the bottom of the pie, or slices of interlarded bacon, and the umbles cut as big as small dice, with some bacon cut in the same form, and seasoned with nutmeg, pepper, and salt, fill your pyes with it, and slices of bacon and butter, close it up and bake it, and liquor it with claret, butter, and stripped tyme.
>
> (May R., 1660)

Samuel Pepys discloses how he enjoyed a dish of Umble pie in his diary entry on 5 July 1662: 'I having some venison given me a day or two ago, and so I had a shoulder roasted, another baked, and the umbles baked in a pie, and all very well done.' And on 8 July 1663: 'Mrs Turner came in and did bring us an Umble-pie hot out of her oven, extraordinarily good.'

*****

A common explanation for offal's fall from favour with the British public is that, unlike other meat, it was rarely rationed during the

Second World War, meaning that people had their fill of offal and it came to be associated with the wartime ethos of making do. When rationing ended in 1954 the public wanted nothing more than to eat the prime cuts they had been denied and had no desire to eat the offal that had been the main meat option.

At the same time global trade was growing rapidly, on a far greater scale than ever before. Britain's increased demand for food supplies led to the intensification of farming and an rise in the marketing of food products. These changes had an impact on the meat trade, and though this may not have been apparent immediately, it was set to completely overhaul the way we ate, shopped and produced food.

Butcher shops and small independent slaughterhouses dramatically declined, while supermarkets and importers began to dominate the industry. Such far-reaching changes had drastic repercussions on consumer tastes, industry relations, the very definition of convenience, and, as a result, offal's popularity and position within our food supply.

The Second World War broke down many established supply networks as the meat trade was nationalised and decentralised to different parts of the country, largely to minimise the impact of bombing. The industry remained under government control well beyond the end of the war. Until 1954 most meat could only be acquired via ration books – or on the black market, where a lucrative trade in rabbit and poultry took place.

The government had to find a way to fulfill this growing demand for meat by improving the packaging and distribution of food being imported to feed the nation. Rapid innovations in cold storage transportation took place, combined with a trend for deboned and 'deglanded' carcass imports which took less space to transport.

These trends had a dire impact on small-scale UK slaughterhouses. Firstly, a rise in the number of imported carcasses – as opposed to animals imported live – meant that they became increasingly redundant. Between the 1950s and 1970s Britain's approximately 5,000 small slaughterhouses decreased to just 110 larger ones.

The butchers, meanwhile, reported that they too began to buy pre-cut meat and less offal as they 'modernised' their stock to try to keep up with the supermarkets and reduce their waste and overheads. Changing systems meant deboned meat could be sold prepared, ready to cook on small trays. In many respects this is the trend that has given rise to people becoming squeamish about 'animal parts' that actually look like they have come from an animal.

Decreasing family sizes, an increase in women working and a trend towards global cuisine all helped towards reinventing the general approach to meat and the fashion for certain cuts. Modern housewives suddenly had a choice of cuts and were no longer so willing to prepare meat themselves. Convenience was now king and shifts in global trade made consumption ever more convenient for the consumer. White, boneless meat from around the world was the desire of the modern working woman – a luxury that was incomprehensible to previous generations of wives and mothers. Whether it was consumer tastes or industry reforms that led the way in bringing about these changes remains in dispute, but it is certain that faced with the option of boiling a cow's stomach or popping a prepared chicken in the oven the latter was seen as more appealing.

The eating habits of British consumers changed once again in the wake of the BSE crisis. Following an extended period of research into the disease the UK government confirmed a link between BSE and Creutzfeldt-Jakob Disease (CJD). The EU banned exports of British beef with effect from March 1996, and offal cuts such as brain, spinal-cord, spleen, thymus, tonsils and intestines had to be stained and disposed of. According to slaughterhouse worker Brian Hewitt, it cost the industry £22 million that year to get rid of this offal. Many went out of business or faced severe financial struggles as a result of the ban. John Brewster described the BSE crisis as the worst disaster ever to hit the industry: 'It was nearly impossible for us to accept the existence of this disease.' He recalls being interviewed on radio and claiming that it was not too serious, but he 'did know in [his] heart of hearts that the sterilisation process involved in animal feed' had become insufficient.

The loss of offal's financial value came about as a result of complex socio-economic shifts, but its cultural value was also lost as new notions of convenience arose alongside increased levels of technology and commerce. Pre-war practices had largely reconciled the interests of slaughter, sale and consumption around an economic use of the whole animal. But the new conveniences now expected by modern households focused on quick, easy and cheap procurement and preparation of meat.

The UK food system has come a long way from the pre-war localised systems of meat production that used every morsel of the animal. Offal's diverse and delicious cuts continue to turn a few food-loving heads, but it is unlikely to slip back into mainstream consumption any time soon. For a generation never encouraged to enjoy the off-cuts as children, it is increasingly difficult to turn them onto the cuts they think of as icky or disgusting. Offal needs to be revalued as safe and beneficial to both the environment and industry. This would ultimately require industry upheaval – a complete rethink of the slaughter and packaging process and a fresh appraisal of meat by-products in the public imagination

Tripe

The French adore it, the Italians greedily devour it and at one time the British could not get enough of it; but it's fair to say that in Britain nowadays tripe doesn't have the best of reputations. Whilst it may have very few calories and be packed with more protein than a piece of steak, very few would relish the thought of tucking into a plate of gelatinous cow's stomach, no matter how well disguised. Indeed, the thought of jellied tripe with a glass of wine in the summer strikes fear into most people.

Tripe generally refers to the stomach lining of various farm animals, most commonly in Britain that of the cow. There are several different types of tripe and they are defined according to the part of the stomach lining they are taken from. Plain tripe comes from the first stomach of the cow, honeycomb the second and bible, or leaf, the third. The fourth stomach is mainly used for the production of rennet with its glandular structure rendering it mainly unsuitable for any other use.

Tripe is usually sold ready cleaned and parboiled and the work of the tripe dresser would have been a laborious one that required a strong constitution. The beef tripes in their raw state are generally various shades of brown, depending on the diet of the animal before slaughter. The tripes are inspected for cysts or other irregularities before being cold-water flushed to remove their digestive contents. The job of tripe dressing is not a quick, clean or pleasant one. Tripe in its raw state has a strong odour that could be likened at best to wet hay or perhaps more accurately to that of a cowshed. Once treated, tripe becomes less aromatic, though it is never neutral in smell. In its untreated, natural state tripe is covered with an impervious protective layer of skin that must be removed before the characteristic creamy coloured tissue is exposed; this was traditionally done by hand with the aid of a dandy brush. The creamy-coloured, denuded tripe requires much washing and scalding before it undergoes a long boil. The length of the boil is dependent upon the tripe dresser's style but also the age of the animal. The snowy white appearance of tripe is achieved by bleaching it in a weak peroxide solution, which also plumps the appearance of the tripe. The tripe is finally rinsed and then checked over, trimmed and 'dressed' for retail.

The preparation and eating of tripe has a long history and was esteemed by both the Greeks and the Romans. In the Middle Ages it is rumoured that William the Conqueror, having made Caen his own signature city, enjoyed partaking in the local speciality *tripes à la modie de Caen*. It is said that this local dish dates back to the medieval period and the original recipe was the idea of a monk from the Men's Abbey in Caen. Legend also has it that the Duke of Normandy and King of England really enjoyed a meal of local tripe, accompanied by apple juice. Cow's stomachs were not just prized for food: a recipe for eye salve found in the Anglo-Saxon medical textbook *Bald's Leechbook* directs that onion, garlic, wine and cow's bile should be crushed together and left in a bronze vessel for nine days and nights. Modern research has actually shown this recipe to be a powerful remedy, and far from being hocus pocus, tests revealed that the eye salve killed MRSA in the lab faster than the most potent modern-day antibiotic.

Tripe is a versatile food and one that has long been celebrated as being easy to digest. In Turkey market workers enjoy tripe soup, and other countries choose to serve it flavoured with herbs and spices. In England the traditional way of eating it is simmered in milk and cooked with onions or else soused in vinegar. In Mrs Beeton's *Book of Household Management* tripe is described as being 'the most digestible of meats, and specially suited for invalids, although rather fat. Sometimes served as an entrée. It consists of paunch or ruminant stomach of the ox.' When thinking of a dish of tripe it conjures up thoughts of a simple supper. Indeed in Charles Dickens' *Barnaby Rudge* one of the characters is rewarded with 'A steaming supper of boiled tripe and onions, to which meal he did ample justice.' It's hard to think of this 'digestible' food as anything more than plain and even though Mrs Beeton's *Book of Household Management* contains a recipe for Fricasseè of Tripe, it essentially boils down to a recipe for tripe cooked in milk with parsley and onions. Elizabeth Raffald's treatment of tripe in her 1769 book *The Experienced English Housekeeper* is even simpler, involving boiling in salted water with onions and serving with parsley and butter.

Tripe eating is so deeply ingrained in our culture that it has even appeared in our literature. Grumio in Shakespeare's *The Taming of the Shrew*, enquires, 'How say you to a fat tripe – finely broiled?'

Whilst in 1662 Samuel Pepys records 'a very great meal' referring to 'a most excellent dish of tripes of my own directing, covered with mustard.' (Pepys, 1957). Clearly, the meal was a success and so perhaps it should be no surprise to see that tripe was worthy of a later entry in his diary: 'Home to dinner on tripes.'

It is certain that when it comes to tripe, there's no middle ground – you either really love it or absolutely detest it. There is no escaping the fact that it is the edible lining from the stomach of cattle or sheep, and whilst throughout the nineteenth century and well into the mid twentieth century it was a popular item on the menu, served on its own, in a salad, with onions, or even in a pie, it gradually fell from grace on British dining tables. It was perhaps just too much for modern diners to stomach.

Despite some attesting to the slimy texture and unpleasant smell of this dish, for others tripe is a great source of gastronomic delight, with some devotees even terming it 'Lancashire calamari'. Tripe was known for being nutritious and a good, honest food; it was even rumoured to boost a man's libido. An advertisement for United Cattle Products (UCP) in the 1920s declared tripe to be perfect for the 'active man': 'As nutritious as red meat, far more easily digested and far more economical, essentially an ideal food for men of energy.'

Perhaps it would be fair to say that tripe has always been an acquired taste. This would explain why the word can be used as a derogatory term to refer to something you believe is silly, false or worthless, for example, 'I've never heard such a load of tripe in all my life,' or 'they're talking tripe', while a 'Tripe-Wife' was a female tripe dresser of dubious character, as demonstrated in the line from Richard Bromes' *City Wit*: 'Was not thy mother a notorious tripe-wife?'

Tripe dressing was a popular trade in the nineteenth century, particularly in the Midlands and the North of England, where its ease of preparation, low cost and nutritional value was appreciated amongst mill workers who were time poor. However, while tripe dressing was undoubtedly a trade that required skill and knowledge, the conditions under which it was sometimes carried out could be less than desirable both from a health and hygiene perspective.

In 1832 James Phillips Kay paints a vivid picture of the filthy conditions in which some tripe dressers were operating in the poor areas of Manchester:

> Pursuing the course of the river on the other side of Ducie Bridge, other tanneries, size manufactories, and tripe-houses occur. The parish burial ground occupies one side of the stream, and a series of courts of the most singular and unhealthy character, the other. Access is obtained to these courts through narrow covered entries from Long Millgate, whence the explorer descends by stone stairs and in one instance by three successive flights of steps to a level with the bed of the river. In this last mentioned (Allen's) court he discovers himself to be surrounded, on one side by a wall of rock, on two others by houses three stories high, and on the fourth by the abrupt and high bank down which he descended, and by walls and houses erected on the summit. These houses were, a short time ago, chiefly inhabited by fringe, silk, and cotton weavers, and winders, and each house contained in general three or four families. An adjoining court (Barrett's,) on the summit of the bank, separated from Allen's court only by a low wall, contained, besides a pig-stye – a tripe manufactory in a low cottage, which was in a state of loathsome filth. Portions of animal matter were decaying in it, and one of the inner rooms was converted into a kennel, and contained a litter of puppies. In the court, on the opposite side, is a tan yard where skins are prepared without bark in open pits, and here is also a catgut manufactory.
>
> (Kay Shuttleworth, 1832)

Tripe dressing here represents not only a 'foul- smelling' process, but seems to be conducted in a most hazardous environment: 'Offal was allowed to accumulate with the grossest neglect of decency and disregard to the health of the surrounding inhabitants.' It is not hard to imagine the dreadful conditions and it's perhaps not surprising that in 1875 tripe boilers, blood boilers, bone boilers and tallow melters were all designated as 'offensive trades', under The Public Health Act and therefore had to be regulated by local or urban district councils. In 1877 the district council of Kearsley published a set of byelaws for activities of tripe boilers which stipulated, 'Every tripe boiler shall adopt the best practicable means of rendering innocuous all vapours during the process of boiling.' Later bylaws made under Section 108 of the Public Health Act, 1936, carried similar wording relating to vapours from tripe boiling diffusing in the air. Burnley Borough Council also addressed the issue of refuse, stating that, 'at the close of every working day, cause all manure, garbage, inedible offal, filth or refuse which has fallen or been deposited upon any part of the premises and is not intended to be forthwith subjected to any further trade process upon the premises to be collected and to be removed from the premises.' These bylaws were designed to reduce the risks to public health and improve the living conditions of those in close proximity to offensive trades. These bylaws were strict and a failure to observe and give full consideration to them resulted in considerable fines.

Many tripe boilers found themselves in court for failing to observe the appropriate bylaws and thus causing a public nuisance. Local newspapers carried stories of 'rogue' tripe dealers and the penalties inflicted upon them. In 1901 one such headline told of the 'intolerable nuisance' that a tripe dresser in Chester was creating:

At the Chester Castle Petty Sessions, on Saturday, Eberhardt Rehfeldt, tripe-dresser [...] was summoned by Chas. J. Owen, sanitary inspector to the Chester Rural District Council, for not abating a nuisance on his premises at Littleton. Mr. Owen [...] visited the place owing to complaints that had been made. They found the whole of the surroundings in a very bad state, especially a ditch [...] The foul stuff from the ditch had polluted a pit. Dr. Kenyon, medical officer of health, said the premises consisted of a small shed in an extremely rough condition, and very imperfectly laid with bricks. There were a ditch and a small pit near, and heaps of manure and filth around about the pigstyes. The quantity of filth there and the filthy nature of the ground was an intolerable nuisance. It was impossible to carry on the business in that locality owing to the absence of drains, the insufficient nature of the building, and the absence of a proper water supply [...] The neighbours complained of the state of the ditch. Mr. Samuel Williams, who resides near the premises, and who, with his landlord, was represented by Mr. Brassey, said the filth percolated through the land and drained into his pit, and he had had to fence it off so that his horses should not drink it. Mr. E. S. Giles, solicitor, said he himself lived opposite the last witness on the Tarvin Road. He knew the premises complained of, and he had not the least hesitation in saying that if tripe-dressing was carried on in the city as it was there, it would be stopped immediately. It was a disgusting nuisance [...] The smell was absolutely intolerable.

(Chester Tripe Dresser Summonsed, 1901)

The insanitary condition of tripe dressers' premises were not the only times that tripe made the headlines. It seems that drunkenness and tripe do not make for a good outcome as the *South Wales Daily News* reported on 6 June 1895:

CHOKED WITH TRIPE A DRUNKEN WOMAN'S END
On Tuesday night, shortly before 12 o'clock, a woman
named Susan George, 53 years of age [...] was choked
to death with a piece of tripe. It appears from the
information received by the police that deceased shortly
after 11 o'clock went upstairs to bed in a drunken state
with a piece of tripe in her hand. Some time after her son
found her in a dying state and sent for Dr Walker, but when
the latter arrived on the scene and made an examination
he found life extinct, and on further investigation it was
found that the windpipe had been choked up with pieces
of tripe.

This was not a solitary case of misadventure by tripe. In May 1889 'Ann
Miles, aged 64 years, who resided at Longlandov Street, Bradford,
was choked by a piece of tripe.' (Choked by Tripe, 1889). Whilst 'an
extraordinary case' was reported in October 1895 in the *Evening
Express* of a woman named Sarah Colyan, who 'was partaking of
a tripe supper, when she showed signs of choking. Some tripe was
taken from her mouth, but she relapsed into unconsciousness, and
was put to bed. Her children slept with her, and one of them early
next morning discovered that the woman was dead. Another- piece
of tripe was found in Colyan's throat.' (Woman choked by Tripe,
1895). Thankfully, not all tripe suppers ended in death, but a liking
for tripe could end in an appearance in court, as it did in the case of
a Blackpool man named Francis Smith who was fined in 1899 for
drunkeness after he was reported 'to have entered a fish and chip
potato restaurant and bought a pound of tripe, taking another pound
himself from the window, besides having three-quarters of a pound
weighed, finishing by drinking two bottles of vinegar and putting
the fish into his pocket.' As if his thirst for vinegar and tripe was
not bizarre enough, the report reads that he 'Then he offered the
shopkeeper a threepenny bit, and asked for change.'

Over time tripe dressers and tripe shops cleaned up their act and employed modern, up-to-date methods to prepare, store and sell tripe. The terrible tales of insanitary tripe traders mainly subsided, and the tripe trade flourished up to and during the Great War. It is undoubtedly the case that the difficult economic climate of the 1930s forced some tripe sellers to closed, but because tripe was upheld as a wholesome and economical dish it meant that even in the face of the slump and great Depression tripe remained a popular dish.

In *Homely Hints and Dainty Dishes*, tripe is heralded for its economical qualities. Entitled 'A Cheap Tripe Dinner', the advice reads:

> Sometimes the cuttings of tripe, or pig's chitterlings, or even a cow heel can be had very cheaply. They should be cut into square pieces. Peel eight good onions and ten large potatoes for every four pounds of the meat. Lay some of the potatoes at the bottom of the pot, season with salt and pepper, then some of the tripe, then onions and potatoes until all is in. Then mix a quarter of a pound of flour with three quarts of water; mix smooth and boil gently for two hours. This will make enough for a family of twelve.
>
> (*For Women Folk: Homely Hints*
> *And Dainty Dishes*, 1906)

Its cheap and nourishing properties saw tripe remain hugely popular in the north of England and in the Midlands up until the late 1970s and tripe stalls were featured in most markets during this period. However, with the emergence of more price competitive alternative foods including frozen and tinned goods and the emergence of more varied takeaway options as well as the rise of microwaves and ready meals the heyday of tripe was in the past. Tripe became an old-fashioned foodstuff that now causes upturned noses and a general lack of excitement. For some reason the idea of eating a meal of hot, steaming cow's belly just doesn't appeal.

Cow's udders

'Elder' is the name given to cooked cow's udder, an offal dish rarely seen today. As a nation that once ate everything, Britain once enjoyed cow's udder, boiled and served cold or fried in butter for supper.

There were more than 260 tripe shops in Manchester alone a century ago, many of which sold elder and it was usual for families to enjoy tripe, elder and other types of offal two or three times a week.

A sandwich of elder would be a welcome treat, yet today the thought of thinly sliced cow's udder liberally seasoned with salt and vinegar might be considered curious or revolting to today's diner. Elder would also be garnished with black pepper, sliced tomato and pickled onion and served with brown bread. It was still a popular dish in the 1920s and 1930s, and so throughout the Second World War, though by the 1950s it had started to decline in popularity amongst the younger generation.

In the heatwave of August 1955, the *Northern Daily Telegraph* reported on the downturn in tripe sales during the traditionally busy hot months. The Women's Editor, in her article about 'today's attitude to the traditional Lancashire dish', reported: 'Half a pound of tripe and two trotters is Grandma's solution to the hot-weather problem of providing cool appetising teas,' but as the article revealed, the trend for offal was on a downwards spiral. Indeed, tripe salad, cold tongue sandwiches and cold elder and jellied veal were all traditional British summer dishes. One Accrington shopkeeper who had enjoyed good sales in the hot summer of 1955 reported, 'We could have sold three times as much tripe as we have been getting in the past few weeks.'

The fifties were giving rise to a new generation that was too stylish and well-to-do for offal, meaning that delicacies such as cow heel, sheep and pig's trotters, cow's udder elder and tripe were going out of favour with those under forty. 'Young housewives turn their noses up at tripe because they seem to think it old-fashioned and not sophisticated enough for them. They certainly wouldn't dream of offering it to guests,' a Burnley tripe-dealer told the *Northern Daily Telegraph* in 1955, and whilst offal remained on menus well into the 1960s its halcyon days were over. The decline of offal consumption is reflected in the decline of tripe dressers and offal dealers. In 1951, in Blackburn alone, there were thirty-two tripe dressers and dealers serving the town's hungry households, but by 1966 their numbers had been cut to just five firms. By 1997 there were just two tripe stalls left on the town's markets; today this is down to just one. Similarly, while Burnley boasted ten tripe companies, wholesale and retail, in 1953, by the late nineties there was just one tripe stall left in the town's market hall and this has now closed its doors.

Today, a few specialist tripe stalls still exist, but it is a far cry from the hundreds of tripe-shops that onCe existed in the Midlands and Lancashire. The UCP, or United Cattle Products, ran a chain of dedicated offal butchers across the north, many of which had cheap nose-to-tail café-restaurants attached.

When cooked, elder has a soft yet firm consistency not unlike cooked liver and was frequently sold either cooked and sliced alongside other cold meats or whole for home cooking (in which case it was usual to boil it or cook it slowly in milk or else stuff and roast it). Elder has a creamy, yellow colour and was sold without being bleached. It was enjoyed with fresh bread and butter in much the same way as pate might be enjoyed today.

Samuel Pepys made an entry in his diary on Thursday, 11 October 1660 that recorded his enjoyment of udder: 'Mr. Creed and I to the Leg in King Street, where he and I, and my Will had a good udder to dinner.' That other great diarist, Parson James Woodforde, was not so impressed with the dish. His entry for 17 February 1763 read, 'I dined at the Chaplain's table with Pickering and Waring, upon a roasted Tongue and Udder [...] N.B. I shall not dine on a roasted Tongue and Udder again soon.'

Parson makes later references to tongue, so it appears that it was the udder that was not to his liking. Indeed, in 1786 he had cold tongue in his cellar which, if nothing else, his dog enjoyed, 'unfortunately the cellar door being left open [...] one of the greyhounds (by name Jigg) got in and eat the whole with a cold tongue etc.'

Udder and tongue were both popular dishes in the seventeenth century and they were featured together in many recipes, including in Hannah Glasse's *The Art Of Cookery Made Plain And Easy*, in which she instructs cooking the tongue and udder together. In Meg Dodds's *The cook and Housewife's Manual* (1826) there is a recipe for boiled tongue that is served sliced and served with tomato or onion sauce or else simmered and salted and served cold with oil and vinegar. Indeed cow's udder was so prized that the royal household ordinances of 1474 record that 'uthers' (and ox-feet) were excluded from the perquisites of the 'purveyors of beeves and muttons', who got to retain the heads and 'entrayles' of the animals they supplied.

In 1615 Gervase Markham includes a recipe for cow udder in *Countrey Contentments, or, The English Hus-wife*, which sounds fancy enough to have appeased even the 1960s offal snobs as it was laced with sugar and cinnamon:

> To roast a Cows Udder
> Take a Cows Udder, and first boyl it well: then stick it thick all over with Cloves: then when it is cold spit it, and lay it on the fire, and and apply it very well with basting of sweet Butter, and when it is sufficiently roasted and brown, then dredg it, and draw it from the fire, take Venegar and Butter, and put it on a chafing dish and coals; and boyl it with white bread crum, till it be thick: then put to it good store Sugar and of Cinnamon, and putting it into a clean dish, lay the Cows Udder therein, and trim the sides of the dish with Sugar, and so serve it up.

Brains

'Have I lived to be carried in a basket like a barrow of
butcher's Offal, and to be thrown in the Thames? Well, if
I be served Such another trick, I'll have my brains ta'en
out and buttered.'

Shakespeare, *The Merry Wives of Windsor* III.v.4-6

The Roman cookery book *Apicius* included brains as the stuffing
for sausages, and in the occasional brain- and egg-enriched pudding
flavoured with rose, wine, or fruit. However, cooking up a feast of
brains is not just an ancient recipe; there are plenty of recipes to be
found in Victorian, Edwardian and even in retro cookbooks today.
In Mrs Beeton's *All About Cookery* (1861), she includes a recipe for
Calves' Brain Cakes, which begins with preparation of the brains:
'Wash the brains under running cold water or in several changes of
water, and remove any clots of blood, loose skin and fibres. Then soak
in cold water for at least 1 hr., changing the water 2 or 3 times.' The
brains are then boiled with sliced onions, sage, salt, lemon juice or
vinegar, and spices before being chopped up and combined with egg.
The finished mixture is spread onto a plate and cooled before being
divided into small cakes, breadcrumbed and fried.

Even with campaigns to promote offal eating, people remain
apprehensive about eating brains. Whilst you may find haggis,
kidneys, liver or even tripe in a supermarket you won't find brain, and
you may not even find it at your local butchers, though pig, sheep and
goats' brain is available from specialty butchers if you are determined
in your search. There isn't much demand for brain in Britain: perhaps
we can't get over its 'visceral' taste.

Faced with the prospect of preparing a brain for the table many
home cooks may feel queasy. The creaminess of cooked brain, which
has the texture of slightly set custard, is off-putting to some modern
palettes, but it was this delicate, soft and creamy texture that saw

brains once being prized and the demands of their careful preparation led to them being considered even more of a delicacy.

Today, we enjoy the luxury of cooking muscle meat that requires minimal preparation, and the thought of cutting away areas of coagulated blood from a blanched calf's brain before slicing it like butter and frying it may seem rather macabre. However, in days past the luxury of squeamishness could ill have been afforded. In the Victorian period the poor were faced with a diet that at best would include cheap offal such as tripe, but could also include slink (prematurely born calves), broxy (diseased sheep) or 'tainted' meat.

The mid-Victorian 'meat famine' that occurred as a result of domestic meat production not being able to keep up with the demands of a fast-increasing, urbanising population, meant that meat was difficult to acquire, especially for the poorest classes. In 1882 it was reported that, 'England has one sheep per head, and one bullock to five people. Thus it is that the States cannot keep up her supplies.' (*Frozen Meat*, 1882).

New and exciting preservation and transportation techniques enabled Britain to work towards remedying the famine situation with new technologies that enabled the British to eat livestock that was reared, slaughtered and processed in the Americas and Australasia. Suddenly meat extracts became store cupboard staples; frozen mutton and corned beef were becoming available and at a more inclusive price. Such innovations led meat consumption per head to increase dramatically, rising from about 39kg per year in the 1850s to 58lb annually by 1914, despite the fact that Britain's population nearly doubled in this period.

The price of meat fell as a result of these foreign imports and mass-marketing campaigns and positive media coverage helped promote these new forms of meat. Victorian commentators celebrated frozen meat's capacity to feed the 'energetic, flesh-fed men' required to sustain 'our workpeople, who eat, we are told, double the meat per head of any population in the world.' (*Frozen Meat*, 1882).

Reports of the success and excellent quality of the meat arriving frozen from overseas were making the headlines. One such article documented the first cargoes of frozen meat to London and subsequent successful deliveries with great enthusiasm:

> The ship Protos landed the two first cargoes of frozen meat in London in 1881 from Australia, and similar arrivals have from time to time been safely delivered. Last week, an experiment, perfectly successful, was made in the arrival of the Dunedin, a sailing ship, with 5,000 carcases of mutton on from New Zealand after a voyage of ninety-nine days. The splendid condition of this meat, and the superb quality it is found to possess, has disturbed certain pessimists who pretend to see this enterprise as another blow dealt at the already tottering English farmer.
>
> (*Frozen Meat*, 1882)

Meanwhile 'beef tea' was widely advertised as a life-enhancing force in Britain's fights against alcoholism and influenza, and was championed as a restorative food source, with one newspaper } reporting, 'Beef-tea is one of the most important in the list of invalid dishes. It is used to stimulate and nourish when the system has need of quick recuperation.' ('The Best Beef Tea', 1910). Another trumpeted the arrival of 'BEEF TEA FOR THE MILLION{S}', explaining that 'It is quite certain that in many homes where beef tea has hitherto been an unattainable luxury it will now become an article of general use, owing to the recent introduction of beef tea in tablet form at the low price of Id. per tablet.' (Beef Tea for the Million, 1907)

Meat remained a luxury for the poorest classes in Victorian Britain. But as the nineteenth century came to a close, and as more and more British consumers grew accustomed to imported beef and mutton, the idea of meat forming the central part of every meal became increasingly popular amongst the working classes as well as middle-class meat eaters. And while controversy raged around the wholesome quality of imported meat and preserved meats there was avid support for the globalisation of meat supply. Advocates of the canning and refrigeration industries championed their capacity to deliver healthy, wholesome, inexpensive and sustainable meat supplies from Britain's colonies and the New World. There was plenty of support for endorsing the quality of imported frozen meat, but also some concerns over the safety of far flung slaughterhouses, as an 1897 newspaper article shows:

> IS FROZEN MEAT WHOLESOME? Science siftings make the following answer to this question certainly most wholesome. It is but vulgar prejudice, sown by the farmers and butchers of this country, to hold that freezing impairs the tasty quality and nutriment of meat. Australian, American, New Zealand meat, all are excellent. Why, then, should grasping middlemen be allowed to de-press the British poor by keeping up the price of meat? There is only one legitimate objection to be brought against the importation of cheap meat – that is, the defective inspection that obtains in foreign or colonial slaughter-houses, involving as it does, much risk of inoculating our frozen-meat eaters with disease. When the needful sanitary measures are enforced, our poor may be freely encouraged to sustain health and strength on a cheap diet of imported meat.
>
> (*Flintshire Observer Mining Journal and General Advertiser for the Counties of Flint Denbigh*, 1897)

Home-reared British meat was generally perceived as being of superior quality and much safer, especially early on in the development of these industries. However, foreign imports of meat were cheaper and for those who were governed by a restrictive budget and used to the hardship of 'tainted' meat, buying 'cat or dog meat' or searching for odds and ends not required by the butcher 'this inferior and much cheaper mutton' was a welcome blessing.

While those who could afford to be picky were put off cheaper meat imports by scandals involving putrefied meat and concerns over its origins, those who were hungry and of limited income could not be mealy mouthed. The import rates continued to increase and no amount of fears relating to foreign farmers palming off offal or meat from diseased animals to Britain, or concerns over freshness, or even worries that boiled human babies were entering the food chain could stop the quell the demand of cheap flesh.

While demands to protect traditional British agriculture were voiced loudly, animal rights campaigners were also concerned at the increasingly intensive farming methods, animal welfare and assembly-line slaughter techniques associated with developing and increasingly intensive meat markets.

Britain's growing vegetarian movement was promoting the economic, health and ethical benefits of a meat-free diet and support was growing for this cause. Writing in the 1886s, the prominent animal rights activist, vegetarian and socialist Henry Stephens Salt exclaimed, 'I think it will be worth our while to inquire if there be really such absurdity in the idea of not eating flesh.' (Salt, *A Plea for Vegetarianism*, 1886). Within his essay, he proceeds to put forward many arguments as to the merits of vegetarianism not least that 'flesh-meat is so much more expensive than cereals or vegetable products that it must be accounted extravagant.' Salt concludes that 'future and wiser generations will look back on the habit of flesh-eating as a strange relic of ignorance and barbarism.'

The Vegetarian Society had seen a decline in membership in the first half of the century, but by 1880 support was increasing, at a time when traditional farming could not meet demand and the world of intensive farming was looming. Poor diet, hunger and malnutrition was a reality for the poor and the prospect of eating frozen meat from the other side of the world inspired worry and revulsion in many. Britain's diet was changing and offal was by no means the most forbidding prospect.

The most deprived urban poor, who lived in slums, had very little access to meat, surviving on thin broths and meagre scraps. The attitude of 'beggars can't be choosers' prevailed and there was no room for indulgent sensibility. The nutritional effects of poor diet were visible: one study found that recruits to the navy from the slums were on average 8.6 inches shorter than the wealthy or middle-class recruits to a Royal Military Academy.

Against the backdrop of shortage and hunger, the prejudice towards eating organs was not entertained by the poorer classes. Brains were seen as a perfectly good meal and graced Britain's tables in many guises. Sheep's innards, gristly bits, and heads could be purchased cheaply and would provide opportunities for bone broths and nutrition. The head in particular provided delightful treats such as nubbins of brain, eyeballs, or tongue.

Whether pickled, fried, boiled or casseroled, brains have been appreciated for their protein-packed properties and eating them remained popular well into the 1930s, appearing in economical cookbooks of the time. So popular were brains that during the Second World War a mock brain recipe was created as a substitute for the real thing. Even offal became difficult to acquire as the war progressed, with most of it being reserved by the butcher for sausage making and what was left being in great demand. The recipe for mock brains called for leftover porridge, onion, herbs, flour and a little egg to be combined. The mixture was then made into patties and fried. The recipe is reflective of the mild flavour and soft texture associated with cooked animal brains, which are often likened to the consistency of scrambled eggs with a creamy finish.

In *Away, Dull Cookery!* Thomas Welby argued the merits of brains as an ingredient: 'we do not make anything like enough use of brains.' Enthusiastically promoting the use of this offal, he continued, 'he value of this delicate, very easily digested and wonderfully restorative article of diet […] can hardly be exaggerated.'

Throughout history brains have been used in recipes for everything from Scottish sheep's brain cakes made with oatmeal through to Elizabeth Raffald's recipe in *The Experienced English Housekeeper* for Calf's Head Hash which is served with Brain Cakes. The heads of sheep, calf and boar have been enjoyed for centuries and were prized for their meaty flavour, while the brains of calves are considered by most to be superior: 'There is scarcely any difference in the flavor,' wrote Charles Fellows in *The Culinary Handbook* (1904). Pickled sheep's brains may not be to everyone's taste, and the instructions for dressing a calf's head that begins with, 'skin the head and split it, take the black part out of the eyes,' may prove a little gory for today's home cook (before even getting to the preparation of brain sauce), but brains have been devoured with delight throughout history and may have been consumed without knowledge in popular recipes such as mock turtle soup. Mock turtle soup was a popular dish created in the eighteenth century using brain, organ meats and calf's foot to make a highly flavoured imitation of the stylish green turtle soup that was popular on the tables of the wealthy. So popular was the recipe for mock turtle soup that companies including Heinz, Cross and Blackwell and Cambell's all produced a tinned version. Heinz continued to produce mock turtle soup in their popular range into the 1960s, alongside kidney soup, which was finally retired in the 1980s.

Animal brains have been traditionally included in recipes for processed pies and meat products. Indeed, the original saveloy was made using pork brains and many British sausages up until the Bovine Spongiform Encephalopathy (BSE) epidemic contained brain, spinal cord and other offal.

When the Bovine Offal (Prohibition) Regulations, 1989, banned high risk beef products, including beef on the bone, from being sold, along with some offal including brain and spinal cord, this spelled a big change to British eating patterns and seemed to strike fear into even the most avid offal advocate.

Today, there is plenty of support for offal to make it back to British dining tables. Indeed celebrity chefs and many corpse-crunching foodies with a liking for heart, liver and lights as well as more unusual offal have all heralded nose to tail eating as being an exacting solution to cutting down on food waste, cutting the cost of grocery shopping and optimizing nutrition. In recent years offal dishes have been rediscovered by acclaimed chefs, and have found their way onto many of the world's finest menus. In 2010 Heston Blumenthal served up an imaginative menu including a starter that was devised to look like a bowl of fruit but was in fact made up of sweetbreads and assorted offal, including brain and testicles. His clients were the Queen and the Duke of Edinburgh who dined with twenty-six of their friends and family at Windsor. Auguste Escoffier's beloved sweetbreads paled into insignificance in comparison to the world's most expensive haggis which caused an offal (sorry) stir in 2016 with its hefty £4,000 price-tag. Made to order, it contained Highland wagyu beef from hand-reared cattle in Perthshire, white summer truffle from France, tellicherry black pepper from India and was decorated with edible 24-carat gold. Weighing 4kg the special haggis was an ode to luxury and was presented in a handmade wooden cask. It was a far cry from the traditional recipe of lamb's pluck (heart, lungs and liver), meat trimmings, suet and oatmeal stuffed in a sheep's stomach. While some offal has become the stuff of fine dining fantasies, and ox cheeks in red wine sauce even made it onto the menus of roadside restaurant chain Little Chef in 2009, it is certain that some offal is still considered too gory to stomach by most modern diners.

Tongues, Trotters, Heads and Chitterlings

On 17 September 1910 butcher Richard Sykes proudly announced that his 'High Class Pork Stores' in Rhyl was the 'The Place for Table

Delicacies' and his list of daily offerings included, 'Old English Boars Head, Tripe, English Ox Tongues, Pressed Pig's Tongue, Oxford brawn, Chitterlings, chawls, feet and eyepieces'. (Richard Sykes Advert, 1910). These were all considered great delicacies a century ago and plenty of other establishments offered similar fare with specialities such as pickled tongue and 'head cheese'.

References to chitterlings, brawn, pigs' trotters, heads and tongues are littered throughout newspapers, cookery books and household manuals, while regional specialities such as Bath chaps seem to have become obscure in recent years. If you happen to have a pig's head floating around that is destined for a stock pot then a dish of Bath chaps could be an elegant addition to your table. The word 'chap' is simply a variant of 'chop', which, in the sixteenth century, meant an animal's jaws and cheeks. Originally the recipe for a Bath chap used the lower portion of a long-jawed pig's cheeks, pickled in brine for up to three weeks, soaked in fresh water for twenty-four hours then boiled for three to four hours. Cooled, skinned and rolled in breadcrumbs, this recipe made the very best of the jaw of the pig, which is fatty. They were traditionally eaten cold with mustard to cut through the fat, or else with eggs as a supper dish. They have long been regarded as a West Country delicacy and were associated with the Gloucester Old Spot, whose long jaw is ideally suited to the cut. As is often the case, the recipe has altered over the centuries and by the nineteenth century meat from both upper and lower jaws was used, though the lower, which contained the tongue, sold at twice the price of the upper and became a more highly prized item.

The tongue from oxen, sheep, calves and pigs have long been pickled, pressed and roasted to offer a culinary treat. Today, when most people think of preparing a supper or an elegant picnic they won't automatically think of cold tongue, yet the riparian feast in *The Wind in the Willows*, was complete with tongue. Spotting the 'fat, wicker luncheon basket', Mole expectantly asked what was inside.

'Oh, there's cold chicken inside it,' replied Ratty, 'Cold tongue, cold ham, cold beef, pickle gherkin salad, French rolls, cress sandwiches, potted meat, ginger beer, lemonade and soda water.' Mole was delighted at the contents of the picnic hamper and was not alone in the relishing the thought of a luncheon of tongue. In her 'Menus for picnics' chapter, Mrs Beeton (*Mrs Beeton's Book of Houshold Management*, 1880) lists tongue on her summer luncheon picnic for twenty persons.

For most, the thought of opening the fridge to find a large, grey, flaccid tongue languishing, all raw and stippled with papillae and marbled with fat is rather horrifying. However, animal's tongues have long been prized for their excellent flavour and texture. Isabella Beeton writes:

> The tongue, whether in the ox or in man, is the seat of the sense of taste. This sense warns the animal against swallowing deleterious substances. Dr. Carpenter says, that, among the lower animals, the instinctive perceptions connected with this sense, are much more remarkable than our own; thus, an omnivorous monkey will seldom touch fruits of a poisonous character, although their taste may be agreeable. However this may be, man's instinct has decided that ox-tongue is better than horse-tongue; nevertheless, the latter is frequently substituted by dishonest dealers for the former. The horse's tongue may be readily distinguished by a spoon-like expansion at its end.
>
> (*Mrs Beeton's Book of Houshold Management*, 1880)

Whether braised in a sauce or served freshly boiled, tongue was a delicacy and featured on many prestigious menus including that for Queen Victoria's New Year's Day dinner served at Osborne House, which also included a boar's head and brawn. There was a time when a simple dish of boiled tongue, glazed and garnished as shown in Mrs Beeton's *Book of Household Management* would have been considered a gourmet delight.

Recipe for Boiled Tongue

Ingredients: 1 tongue, a bunch of savoury herbs, water.

In choosing a tongue, ascertain how long it has been dried or pickled, and select one with a smooth skin, which denotes its being young and tender. If a dried one, and rather hard, soak it at least for 12 hours previous to cooking it; if, however, it is fresh from the pickle, 2 or 3 hours will be sufficient for it to remain in sock. Put the tongue in a stewpan with plenty of cold water and a bunch of savoury herbs; let it gradually come to a boil, skim well and simmer very gently until tender. Peel off the skin, garnish with tufts of cauliflowers or Brussels sprouts, and serve. Boiled tongue is frequently sent to table with boiled poultry, instead of ham, and is, by many persons, preferred. If to serve cold, peel it, fasten it down to a piece of board by sticking a fork through the root, and another through the top, to straighten it. When cold, glaze it, and put a paper ruche round the root, and garnish with tufts of parsley.

If you are not fancying tongue for tea and are erring towards a fish supper then you may want to prepare your fish carefully, as one creature that loves tongue is *Cymothoa exigua*. It enters a fish through its gills, attaches itself to its tongue, then eats away the tongue and effectively becomes the fish's new tongue, surviving on fish mucus, blood and anything the fish eats. It is the only known parasite that replaces an entire organ of its host species, in this case, the poor fish's tongue. They have been commonly found in the mouths of fish purchased from supermarkets and fishmongers, and many cooks preparing a fish dish have been getting a rather nasty surprise. However, *Cymothoa exigua* are not harmful to humans and the most they will do to a human whilst still alive is bite.

*****

Brawn was another popular dish which was served cold or at room temperature, often with mustard. Also commonly called head cheese, this dish was made from pork and bones spiced, boiled and set to cool in molds to form a meaty, jellied terrine. Home-cured pork, fresh-canned pork, sausage, pudding, scrapple, etc, and lard afford a variety of products to supplement the daily meals.

The eighteenth-century household manual *Dictionarium Domesticum* (1736) includes recipes for chitterlings, head cheese, feet and ears. However, before you can make head cheese you must prepare your pig and advice on this is duly given. Under the heading 'BRAWN', it recommends, 'For this you fhould make choice of an old boar, for the older he is, the more horny will the brawn be.' Then detailed instructions on how to prepare your pig so that he is suitable for brawn follow:

> He muft be fed plentifully with peas, as many as he will eat, and fkimnfd milk or flitten milk. This mud be done till he declines his meat, or eats but a very little of it, and then the peas muft be left off, and he muft be fed with pafte, made of barley meal, made up into balls as big as large hens eggs; but ftill continue to give him fkim milk, and in a little time you will find he declines that likewife, which when he does, he is then fit to be killed for brawn.
>
> (1736, p125)

The advice is clear when it comes to making 'brawn of a pig', 'Let the pig be pretty large and fat.' Whilst regional differences exist in recipes, all recipes involve cleaning your pig's head and removing dirt, wax and bristles from it before boiling it for several hours and moulding the resultant gelatinous meat in a slab of its own jelly. In the North East it was often dyed red to give it a more appetizing appearance and some recipes also include other offal including pig's trotters.

May Byron's recipe includes the pigs head, tongue and feet:

> BRAWN (Staffordshire) Take half a pig's head, with the tongue and two feet. Rub it all with salt and pepper and let it be a few days, rubbing well and turning every day. Then boil very gently until the meat comes easily off the bones. Take it out of the saucepan, put it on a board, and cut it all up into rather small pieces, then season with pepper and salt, and press it into a mould or proper brawn tin with holes at the bottom to let the gravy escape, and put a heavy weight on the top. Turn it out when cold, and send to table cold.
>
> (Byron, 1914)

Mrs Beeton's recipe, meanwhile, combines pig's head, less its cheeks' with beef and spices:

> To a pig's head weighing 6 lbs. allow 1 1/2 lb. lean beef, 2 tablespoonfuls of salt, 2 teaspoonfuls of pepper, a little cayenne, 6 pounded cloves. Mode – Cut off the cheeks and salt them, unless the head be small, when all may be used. After carefully cleaning the head, put it on in sufficient cold water to cover it, with the beef, and skim it just before it boils. A head weighing 6 lbs. will require boiling from 2 to 3 hours. When sufficiently boiled to come off the bones easily, put it into a hot pan, remove the bones, and chop the meat with a sharp knife before the fire,

together with the beef. It is necessary to do this as quickly as possible to prevent the fat settling in it. Sprinkle in the seasoning, which should have been previously mixed. Stir it well and put it quickly into a brawn-tin if you have one; if not, a cake-tin or mould will answer the purpose, if the meat is well pressed with weights, which must not be removed for several hours. When quite cold, dip the tin into boiling water for a minute or two, and the preparation will turn out and be fit for use. Time – from 2 to 12 hours. Average cost, for a pig's head, 4 1/2 d. per lb. Seasonable from September to March.

(Mrs Beeton's Housekeeping Book, 1865)

Some recipes include the eyes, brains snout and skin; others the addition of other body parts and, of course, seasoning is always down to personal preference. Some recipes suggest boiling the head and its contents in a stock of herbs and root vegetables; others are selective on which bits of the head should be incorporated; but it seems to be commonly agreed that the ears should be removed, perhaps because they were considered a delicacy in their own right or more probably because they were renowned for being hairy and waxy.

Though recipes for brawn are varied they follow a common theme. An American farmer's bulletin from 1921 recommends a more intense process than most British recipes, instructing that the head be cut into four pieces and soaked overnight before beginning the boiling process:

Cut a hog's head into four pieces. Remove the brains, ears, skin, snout, and eyes. Cut off the fattest parts for lard. Put the lean and bony parts to soak overnight in cold water in order to extract the blood and dirt. When the head is cleaned put it over the fire to boil, using water enough to cover it. Boil until the meat separates readily from the bones. Then remove from the fire and pick out all the bones. Drain off the liquor, saving a part of it for future use. Chop the meat fine with a chopping knife. Return it to the kettle and pour on enough of the liquid to cover the meat. Let it boil slowly for 15 to 30 minutes. Season to taste with salt and pepper just before removing it from the fire. Bay leaves, a little ground cloves, and allspice may be added and boiled for awhile in the soup.

(*Farmer's Bulletin*, 1921)

Cheap brawn was readily in butchers and grocers stores. A slice of cold brawn on a sandwich or on a plate with salad may sound innocuous enough, but from sensational headlines of deaths, poisonings and talk of 'baby's toes', brawn has enjoyed far more than its fair share of notoriety.

In 1906, the headline simply read, 'Baby's Toes' and the story proceeded to tell of how Mr. S. J. L. Vincent, borough surveyor of Newbury, had been given cause to examine a specimen of brawn as it was suggested that it was part of a baby's foot. 'In appearance', said the report, 'this specimen was not unlike the five toes of an infant's foot, or what an infant's toes might be expected to look like after prolonged boiling.' The specimen in question had come from a tin of brawn and no doubt gave rise to alarm upon discovery. However, it did prove to be a false alarm and Mrs Vincent concluded, 'I have now no doubt as to the nature of specimen. It appears to have been a portion of the hard palate of a pig, comprising five ridges with free and rounded alveolar margins, which after cooking sufficiently resembled toes to give rise to the suspicion which was entertained.' (Baby's Toes Brawn, 1906)

Sadly, not all the headlines concerning the safety of eating brawn were wrongly attributed. Death and poisoning as a result of consuming brawn were recurrent. In 1870 a press association telegram read:

The family of a man named Stivens of Leicester, and five other families in the town have been almost poisoned by eating some coloured brawn, which is supposed to have been made of putrefied meat. The magistrates yesterday ordered the shop of the man who sold the brawn to be searched, and further proceedings are to be taken. A later dispatch says one of the sufferers who were poisoned by partaking of the poisoned brawn at Leicester, lies in a promious [sic] condition [...] Seven families, including about 20 children, have suffered from partaking of it.

On 4 September 1886 a tale of the Corpse family, 'eating unwholesome brawn' broke. (Unwholesome Brawn, 1886). The family were described as having, 'narrowly escaped death through eating a quantity of unwholesome brawn.' The brawn had been 'purchased of a butcher in the local shambles, and the whole family partook of it for breakfast. They were very soon afterwards seized with violent pains in the stomach, intense cramps in the abdomen, and excessive and protracted retching.' Some people found that pork brawn was far more perilous, as in the Burry Port Brawn case of 1893 in which there were two fatalities.

Such headlines are perhaps not surprising in light of some of the malpractices of butchers and producers who had a keen eye on their profit margins. On 11 March 1885 a Leicestershire butcher named James Selvidge was charged with 'exposing bad meat for sale,' (Manufacture of Brawn, 1885) after an inspector discovered three cwt. (approx. 152kg) of diseased meat prepared in pickle and destined for brawn on his premises. This was 'in addition to the carcase of a sheep which had suffered from rot, and about a hundred pieces of diseased beef.' Selvidgewas not a first time offender, and neither was he alone in peddling diseased and decomposing meat. There were many other offenders, including George Tyrrell, a provision merchant in Camberwell. In August 1906 Tyrell was fined

20 shillings, and ten guineas costs for having 160 tons of meat that was unfit for human consumption in his possession: 'The meat consisted of German sausages, polonies, saveloys, collard head. and brawn. In the brawn there was found an abscess cavity.' During the hearing it was explained by an expert that the abscess cavity discovered in the brawn meant that 'there was no doubt that the animal from which the meat was obtained was diseased. ('Diseased Meat as Brawn', 1906). In 1910 John Elias Jones, a grocer from Caernarfon, Wales, was summoned under the Food and Drugs Act for selling, 'brawn which contained bristles, a certain bacillus, and a quantity of preservative.' A sample of Mr Jones' brawn was analysed and it was concluded that the sample was 'a very dirty one, contained a large number of bristles, one gramme of bacillus coli communis, and equal to 30.8 grains per lb. of boric preservative.' It was concluded that 'the bacillus found in the sample led to fermentation and putrefaction, and any food containing it was unfit for human consumption. ' ('Bristles in Brawn', 1910)

Even homemade brawn could prove troublesome. One notable case was in 1908, under the headline, 'DEADLY BRAWN', (1908). In a case that was termed 'remarkable', seventeen people from the village of Murrow, Cambridgeshire, were poisoned by eating brawn, two of whom died: 'Mrs Boston, the wife of a bricklayer, bought in the village a quantity of pig bones and a pig's head for the purpose of making brawn, the local name of which is pork-cheese.' Her family members and visitors partook of the brawn. Muriel May Ramsey, aged nine, and Mrs Turner, aged seventy-four, succumbed and another fifteen were taken ill. An inquest held in the fatal cases recorded a verdict of death due to the irritant poison effects caused by eating pork-cheese. It is certain that Mrs Boston would have regretted preparing this pork inspired last supper as a further headline entitled, 'DEATH AFTER EATING BRAWN' told of her demise: 'After making satisfactory progress, Mrs Boston, the woman who made pork cheese or brawn which led to two deaths at Murrow, Cambridgeshire, has died.

About a dozen people are still suffering from the effects of eating the brawn.' (Death After Eating Brawn, 1908)

The perils of eating pork brawn became well known as a series of such cases were attributed to the effects of eating brawn affected with ptomaines. Tinned brawn was no better with similar reports of those who indulged in the canned variety. Such cases, however, did not curb the appetite to any great degree, though perhaps it did make people question the integrity of their brawn purveyors.

If the possibility of poisoning by pork was a risk that seemed too great then there was no need to miss out on a meaty feast of head. Hannah Glasse's recipe for 'Calf's Head Surprize' instructs cooks to 'Take a calf's head with the skin on, take a sharp knife and raise off the skin with as much meat from the bone as you can possibly get, so that it may appear like a whole head when stuffed.' Once you have assiduously removed the skin and meat from the bone, Glasse directs the reader to 'Stuff the head with ingredients including beef suet, veal, bacon and herbs,' before putting the whole thing in the oven for two and a half hours. If this proves too complicated then Glasse offers other recipes including stuffed and boiled calf's head split into three, and arranged on a dish and covered with gravy.

During the Georgian period pig's and calf's heads were often enjoyed simply boiled, baked or hashed, but Glasse offers a wonderfully elegant pie in which to enjoy and relish your calf's head, complete with the eyes.

> To make a Calf's Head Pye
> Cleanse your head very well, and boil it till it is tender, then carefully take off the Flesh as whole as you can, take out the Eyes and slice the Tongue; make a good Puff-paste Crust, cover the Dish, lay in your Meat, throw over it the Tongue, lay the Eyes cut in two, at each Corner; season it with a very little Pepper and Salt, pour in half a pint of the Liquor it was boiled in, lay a thin Top-Crust on,

and bake it in an Hour in a quick Oven. In the meantime boil the Bones of the Head in two Quarts of the Liquor, with two or three Blades of Mace, Half a Quarter of an Ounce of whole Pepper, a large Onion, and a Bundle of Sweet Herbs. Let it boil till there is about a Pint, then strain it off, and add two Spoonfuls of Catchup, three of Red Wine, a Piece of Butter, as big as a Walnut, rolled in Flour, Half an Ounce of Truffles and Morels; season with Salt to your Palate; boil it and have Half the Brains boiled with some Sage, beat them, and twelve Leaves of Sage chopped fine; Stir all together, and give it a boil; take the other Part of the Brains, and beat them up with some of the Sage chopped fine, a little Lemon-peel minced fine, and half a small Nutmeg grated. Beat it up with an Egg, and fry it in little Cakes of a fine Light brown, boil six Eggs hard, take only the Yolks; when your Pye comes out of the Oven, take off the Lid, lay the Eggs and Cakes over it, and pour the Sauce all over. Send it to Table hot without the Lid. This is a fine Dish, you may put in as many fine Things as you please, but it wants no more Addition.

(Glasse, 1793)

Pig's ears

You may not be able to make a silk purse from a sow's ear, but you can make supper out of one, if you should choose to do so.

Today pig's ears are not widely eaten as a standalone dish in Britain. Perhaps the crunchy cartilage and the gelatinous skin in unappealing or perhaps it is the preparation that is considered rather revolting. The ears need to be handled considerably as they are cleaned, the hair is removed and wax is scraped. Even if you buy ears that have been thoroughly cleaned by a butcher you still need to scrape them, singe or pluck them, wash, blanch, skim away the scum and wash them again. After this they are ready to be boiled, for a few hours with or without the rest of the head, and served with some vinegar, or breadcrumbed and fried. They can also be cooked in milk or a white sauce with herbs and spices and served sliced with pig's trotters. Mrs Beeton suggests simmering prepared ears and feet with onion, mace, lemon rind and salt and pepper. Once tender, Beeton directs the home cook to 'cut the feet into neat pieces, and the ears into thin strips' before serving 'thoroughly hot'.

No matter how it is cooked, perhaps the real issue with this piece of offal is that there is just no escaping the fact that it is an ear.

Feet and Trotters

> Check all your razors and your guns
> We gonna be arrested when the wagon comes
> I wanna pigfoot and a bottle of beer
> Send me cause I don't care
> Blame me cause I don't care
> Gimme a pigfoot and a bottle of beer.
> *Gimme A Pig Foot (And A Bottle of Beer)*,
> Bessie James (1933)

Feet represent endless culinary possibilities in the world of offal delicacies. Pig's trotters are rich in gelatine and are usually cooked and eaten hot with vinegar or else stuffed and served steaming hot. Calf's feet are those normally used to make jelly or else thicken broth, and lamb's are served in many different ways: in salads and sauces, or breadcrumbed and grilled.

Pig's trotters were once a popular dish in Britain dish owing to them being cheap, nourishing and easy to prepare. Recipe books were once bulging with details of how to prepare the humble pig's trotter, but its popularity declined as the cheap cut came to be viewed as 'not good enough'.

Pig's trotters are not the prettiest of dishes. Uncooked they are unmistakably recognisable and when cooked have a soft, flabby appearance that can be daunting. Pig's trotters require a long slow cook and most recipes call for boiling or stewing, often with herbs and onions, and enjoyed with the heat of mustard to cut through the fattiness of the dish. This Victorian recipe from America is very typical of the classic and simple way of cooking trotters:

Pig's Feet With Onions
Four boiled pig's feet; two onions; one tea- spoonful of made mustard; two ounces of butter; one tea- spoonful of flour.

Directions – Split the feet in halves; egg and breadcrumb them and broil them; cut the ears into fillets; put them into a double boiler, with two sliced onions, the butter, and the flour. When they are browned, take them up, add the mustard, and lay them on a hot dish. Put the feet on the top of them, and serve.

(Brothers, 1882)

Mrs Beeton offers similar recipes in her *Book of Household Management*, listing recipes for boiled pig's feet, but she also offers a rather more elaborate dish that would serve as an excellent cold supper and would surely elevate pig's trotters to a better class of dining table:

PIG'S FEET AND EARS IN JELLY (*Fr.—Pieds de Pore en Aspic*)

Ingredients — 4 pig's feet, 2 pig's ears, 1 dessertspoonful of finely-chopped parsley, ½ a dessertspoonful of finely-chopped fresh sage, salt and pepper.

Method — Thoroughly cleanse the feet and ears, cover them with cold water, and simmer gently until the bones can be easily withdrawn. Cut the meat into dice, replace it in the liquor, add the parsley, sage, and salt and pepper to taste. Simmer gently for 15 minutes, then turn into a mould or basin, and put aside until cold.

(*Mrs Beeton's Book of Household Managemment,* 1861)

The Dingens Brothers offer in excess of thirty recipes to cook pig's feet, but they also offered some advice on the cooking of calf's feet: 'Calves' Heads and Feet Are generally sold cheap. They are healthy, nutritious, and palatable when cooked properly. If you buy them uncleaned, dip the head and feet into scalding water, with a little rosin added to it; remove the hair and scrape well. After the head is cleaned, cut it open, take out the brains and eyes, let it soak all night in cold water, and cook as per recipes.' One such recipe was Mock Turtle of Calf's Head.

In Britain calves' feet were used in recipes for terrines, soups and stews as well as being used in the popular calf's foot jelly, which was heralded as being a highly nutritious dish and was sweetened and flavoured as a pudding or served as a nourishing savoury dish to the weak or infirm.

Novelist Elizabeth Gaskell revealed how calf's foot jelly was seen as the ultimate comfort food in the nineteenth century, writing in her novel, *My Lady Ludlow*: 'Her way of comforting me was hurrying away for some kind of tempting or strengthening food – a basin of melted calves-foot jelly was, I am sure she thought, a cure for every woe.'

Calf's foot jelly was sold in chemists as a food for invalids and many adverts circulated promoting its health benefits. Recipes appeared not only in cook books but from medical practitioners. One such recipe appeared in 1887:

HOW TO MAKE CALF'S-FOOT JELLY
Procure two calf's feet or a cow-heel, the latter being much cheaper and equally nourishing. Buy two feet with the hair

on, because when ready prepared a deal of the substance which makes jelly has been boiled away. In order to get the hair off, have ready a saucepan of boiling water hold the foot in it with your fingers so that the water just covers the hair; from five to ten minutes is long enough the hair will scrape off easily with a knife. Put the feet into about five pints of water, and boil them till half the water is wasted; strain it, and when cold take off the fat. Put it into a saucepan with sugar, lemon-juice, some lemon-peel, according to taste. If wine is permitted, you will put in as much as is judicious. In order to clear the jelly, the whites of five eggs well beaten up to a froth and the shell broken and must be added. Set the jelly on the fire, but do not stir it after it begins to warm; when it rise to a head, let it boil for twenty minutes. Prepare a conical bag of coarse flannel, with two strings on the broad part, with which to tie it to the backs of two chairs. A course hucka-back towel, which may be tacked together, making one corner the point, is even a better jelly- bag. Dip the bag in hot water, and squeeze it dry. Having placed a basin or shape under the point of the bag, pour the contents of the sauce- pan carefully into it, and they will run slowly through into the shape. Do not press the bag, or the jelly will be cloudy. Great clearness is not important, since this Quality is more to please the eye than the palate. Calf s-foot jelly may be made without wine.

(From *The Family Physician,* January 1887)

Annabella Plumbtre, the daughter of a doctor, included calf's foot jelly in her innovative cookbook that was designed to 'temper instead of pamper the appetite' (Plumbtre, 1813). Recipes including calf's foot jelly, green pudding, fried tripe, herb porridge, tongue, boiled calf's head, cow's udder and roasted eel with lemon juice were promoted for their health giving qualities.

Alongside recipes including a 'Beggar's Pudding', which is made of old scraps of bread soaked in hot water, Plumbtre offers curious health tips which includes advising readers with constipation to drink old sour milk. This is known as 'Boniclapper' and is described as a 'thick slippery substance' designed to 'powerfully open the breast and passages.'

Creating a calf's foot jelly from scratch was not a task for the faint-hearted. It took time and attention, as this 1896 article advertising Clarnico Table Jelly (which was made from calf's foot gelatine) attests:

> Most of us can remember the time when the preparation and making of calves-foot-jelly was quite an event. The feet had to be ordered from the batcher's some time beforehand. These usually arrived with the hair on if not, they had at any rate to be scalded, then boiled for six or seven hours, and allowed to stand all night, before the real work of clarifying and flavouring was even begun. The difficulties of the jelly-bag have long been considered by cooks one of the great drawbacks to jelly-making nor is this to be wondered at when the amount of labour entailed is considered.
>
> ('Jelly that Jells', 1896)

As calf's foot jelly was desirable for the dinner table as well as for the invalid's tray, it is not surprising to find that commercially prepared jelly was popular. An advert for Crosse and Blackwell products that appeared in *Shilling Cookery for the People* reads: 'Calves' Feet Jellies – Consisting of Orange, Lemon, Noyau, Punch, Madiera, and Calf's Foot. These are sold in convenient sized bottles, and their use is attended with a great saving of trouble and inconvenience; besides which, they ensure the certainty of the Jelly always being of uniform excellence and flavour. They are now in almost daily consumption in many families, and are very highly approved.' (Soyer, 1854).

Mary Randolph, in *The Virginia Housewife*, features a detailed recipe for calf's feet jelly and explains that other animal feet can also be utilised: 'The feet of hogs make the palest coloured jelly; those of sheep are a beautiful amber-colour, when prepared.' (Randolph, 1848).

Sheep's trotters were also popular, not just for use in jelly for their lovely hue, but as a good, hot meal. Cooked in much the same way as tripe, these were usually bleached white by tripe dressers to give them a more appealing look. This was not a practice that was employed in the sale of pig's trotters as they naturally had a pale pink colour.

In *A Plain Cookery Book for the Working Classes* Francatelli says:

> Sheep's trotters are sold ready cleaned and very cheap at all tripe shops. When about to cook them, by way of a treat, for supper, or otherwise, let them be put on in two quarts of water and milk, seasoned with peppercorns, salt, a good sprig of thyme, and a wine-glassful of vinegar, and set them to boil very gently on the fire for three hours, at least. When the trotters are done quite tender, skim off all the grease, and boil down the liquor to a pint; then add two ounces of flour, mixed with a gill of milk, some chopped parsley, and one ounce of butter; stir all together while boiling on the fire for ten minutes, and pour out into the dish.
>
> (Francatelli, 1852)

Kelly includes a recipe, dated 1830, in *Good Things in England*, which sees the sheep's feet boiled in stock with 'sweet herbs' and served up with lemon juice or vinegar. She also includes an anecdote about the ritualistic eating of these feet: 'A Bolton lady writes, "we eat sheep's trotters boiled in Bolton, it is a sort of ritual. When the Football Wanderers bring home the Cup, they are received with sheep's trotters decorated with white and blue ribbons".' (Kelly, 1823).

Sheep's trotters were made into soup and broths, and, treated simply, they were seen as a good working-class staple food. However, just like pig's trotters they could be prepared more elaborately for the more discerning palate. In *The Cook's Own Book, And Housekeeper's Register*, (Lee, 1854) there is a recipe for fried sheep's trotters and also one for stuffed trotters which is served with a cream sauce:

> *Sheep's Trotters Stuffed*
> Boil the feet in good stock till the bones will come out with ease; fill the space left by them with a good fowl or chicken farce; dip them in lard, bread them well, and bake in a moderate oven. The space left by the bones is sometimes filled up with a bit of fried bread; in this case the feet are only previously boiled, and then served with cream sauce.

Cow heels were also enjoyed and were often sold ready cooked as a snack or in pies. The United Cattle Products Ltd (UCP) shops advertised that they were 'supplied with tripe and cowheels – fresh daily'. Cow heels were used to enrich gravies, make stews, and because they were rich in gelatinous jelly they proved invaluable in the making of terrines, brawn and potted meats. 'Tripe and cowheels are delicious served hot,' was the message of UCP and they were proclaimed to be 'easy on digestion,' and 'easy on the purse'.

Recipes for cow heel appear in many Georgian cookbooks as they were prized for it taste and economy. They were frequently served with horseradish or strong mustard, although for the more diligent cook they could be served with Mr Michael Kelly's 'Sauce for Boiled Tripe, Calf Head or Calf Heel': 'Garlick vinegar, a tablespoonful – of mustard, brown sugar & black pepper, a teaspoonful each stirred into half a pint of oiled melted butter.' (Lee, 1854). If boiled cow heel didn't appeal there were also recipes for cow heel jellies and for adding chopped cow heel to sweet suet puddings.

71

Cow heel continued to be popular and with an average price of 8d a pound in 1957, it was a well-established everyday food. Recipes for cow heel and steak pies featured in regional newspapers using beef shin, cow heel, onion and seasoning in a suet pastry. Termed as a 'Winter build 'em up' dish, the UCP sold plenty of them in their shops and restaurants, using the slogan 'What About a Cowheel Pie Today?'

The tradition of eating feet in Britain has faded over the years, along with plenty of other offal, so perhaps the thought of eating an animals feet is just not appetizing anymore.

Chitterlings

The meaning of the term chitterlings seems somewhat lost in modern Britain. Chitterlings are also referred to as chidling, chitling, chitter and chitteril and are the washed intestines of an animal that has been prepared and cooked. Usually sold cooked and chilled, sometimes in their own jelly, they are enjoyed cold with vinegar and mustard or else prepared with bacon or veal.

In recent years the term chitterling generally refers to the small intestines of pigs, but originally it also referred to those of ducks and sheep.Very few people visit the butchers today to buy a string of chitterlings; they belong to a time when faggots, dripping, brains, tripe and cow's heel were all standard cuisine. Butchers looked very different in this era, and offered a far wider variety of compared to the indistinguishable muscle meats that are the main stay of a butcher's display today.

In his autobiography, Fred Slater writes of his childhood in the West Midlands: 'On Friday afternoons in Darlaston there were queues of people carrying pots and basins outside Bailey's Pork Butchers, waiting for hot tubs of chitterlings to arrive. Anatomically these are the cleaned and boiled small intestines of pigs, delicious eaten with really hot English mustard [...] Cow's udder, chickens' feet and pigs' trotters were always for sale in the 1940s and 1950s.' (Slater, 2016).

Butcher's shops have changed dramatically in appearance in the past fifty years. Today, aesthetics are everything with modern sensibilities demanding that meat be displayed in neatly wrapped little packages like the ones you find in supermarkets, unlike the Victorian butcher who proudly displayed his vast array of animal carcasses. Butchers also used to either run their own small abattoirs or receive regular deliveries of whole pig, sheep and cow carcasses which would proudly hang in their window displays or outside their shop, along with poultry and game.

This centuries-old tradition of butchers displaying their wares in the window has gradually dwindled. People no longer wish to see severed heads, carcasses and dismembered body parts on display. Many modern diners prefer to protect themselves from the reality of where their meat originates from. There is a disconnection from the reality of what meat truly is that allows bacon sandwiches and sausages to be consumed without thinking about what pork is and that a pig sacrificed its life in the making of that string of sausages in the butchers. Somehow the thought of dead animals for food is considered gruesome.

Once upon a time displays of plucked fowl and the sawn-in-half bodies of pigs and cows pierced on hanging hooks dominated the walls of a butchers and they were proud of their skills and their produce. A wider range of cuts and offal were available and during the festive season and creative and tantalising displays were created to entice customers. Some displays were so magnificent that they were reported on in the local papers, and these reports would include where the meat had been sourced from and any prizes it might have won. A newspaper report from North Wales captured the excitement of shopping in the final few days before Christmas: 'The trades people of the town made fine displays with their Christmas stocks on Tuesday evening and Wednesday. Although very damp underfoot, large crowds of sightseers turned out to witness the show, and throughout Tuesday evening the town was alive with the splendid illumination of the shops, and the gay laughter of youngsters, with whom it is a night of nights.' The feature went on to advise where to shop at Christmas and provided a description of some of the local butchers and their stocks:

> The shop of Mr Robert Roberts, Tan- rhiw and Druid Buildings, Denbigh, was well stocked, including a bullock fed by Mr Cadwaladr Hughes, Glasmir; also a first prize bullock fed by Mr John Jones, Segrwd and first prize Welsh wethers fed by Alderman Job a Roberts, Pias Heaton Farm; home-fed wethers, lambs, and gimmers, and a number of splendid geese. Mr Roberts, butcher, Bridge-street, had a good stock, including a heifer fed by Mr Foulkes, Pencre Felin, and wethers and lambs fed by Mr R Roberts, Foxhall [...] Mrs Parry, butcher, Bridge-street, had a magnificent, show of beef, mutton, pork, etc., which had been fed by several of the principal breeders in the district, including Mr Jones, Cwm Mr Davey, Maesmynan; Mr Lloyd Denton, Ruthin. She had also a tempting variety and selection of home- made pies, brawn, pressed beef, etc., etc. Mr David Roberts' stall in the Market- hall had also a good display of all kinds of meat, the breeders including Mr Davey, Maesmynan, and Mr Jones, Cwm. His stail was well visited. Mr Samuel Roberts, butcher, Vale-street, had, as usual, his shop brightly lit up, and a large and prime stock of Christmas fed meat.
>
> (1910)

How meat is displayed and sold is highly influential on what we serve with our two veg. Neat, tidy and sanitised pieces of muscle meat is what the consumer has been erring towards since supermarkets began to replace traditional butchers. While The Wurzels sang their chitling song the reality was that such offal was already beginning to be considered undesirable by modern diners:

> *Chitterling, chitterling, chitterling*
> *Chitterling is all I crave*
> *Fill me up with chitterling*
> *Think of all the cash you'll save.*
>
> (Chitterling Song, 1971)

While Hannah Glasse gave instructions on how to prepare calf's chitterlings (Glasse, 1793) and Elizabeth Raffald gave instructions on how to prepare many offal dishes in *The Experienced English Housekeeper* (1769), the fact remains that offal has been sliding off the menu for some time. Indeed, today, the feast of Mr Leopold would be viewed as abhorrent: 'Mr Leopold Bloom ate with relish the inner organs of beasts and fowls. He liked thick giblet soup, nutty gizzards, a stuffed roast heart, liverslices fried with crustcrumbs, fried hencods' roes. Most of all he liked grilled mutton kidneys which gave to is palate a fine tang of faintly scented urine.' (James Joyce, *Ulysses*, 1922).

Palates

Palates were very popular in the past and have been used in country and genteel cooking throughout the ages. There are several recipes for them, in the *Larousse Gastronomique*, including a 1769 French recipe for '*Allumettes de Palais de Boeuf*', thin strips of palate which are battered then fried. Hannah Glasse, in her 1747 book *The art of cookery made plain and easy*, includes various recipes for palates, including to stew ox palates, to ragoo ox palates, to fricassée ox palates, to roast ox palates and to pickle ox palates, while Joseph Cooper, in his 1654 book *The Art of Cookery Refined and Augmented*, gives a recipe for Ox Palate Pie.

While stewed ox palate may have been considered an excellent dish in the times of Mrs Beeton, they are no longer used today, but if you were to find them, this is how to prepare them simply according to an excellent recipe from 1874:

Ox palate
Ingredients:
Ox palate
Bouquet garni
Butter
Onion
Carrot
Stock

Blanch for ten minutes an ox palate, drain it, remove the fat, and scrape it carefully; divide it into two parts, and put the palate into a small stewpan with a pint of stock, half an ounce of butter, a little pepper and salt, a bouquet garni, a small onion, and a small carrot. Let the contents simmer for three hours; remove the palate to a cloth, then clean way any fat, and dish with sharp sauce.

(Buckmaster, 1874)

Genitals

Britain has a long history of eating testicles and recipes for their cooking appear in the works of Hannah Glasse and Mrs Beeton, amongst others. You could be forgiven for not knowing that the 'stones' referred to in Elizabeth Hammond's eighteenth-century recipe for Lambstone Pie were testicles. In this recipe the testicles were blanched and sliced and mixed with artichokes and sweetbreads.

The British are not alone in giving animal testicals 'pet' names. The Italians call them *gioielli* ('jewels') or *animelle*, while the French alternate between *les joyeuses* ('the happy ones', in the feminine), *animelles* or *amourettes* ('darling ones' or 'little loves').

The Americans refer to them as 'prairie' or 'mountain oysters', also as 'Montana tendergroins', 'cowboy caviar', 'swinging beef', and 'calf fries'.

Recipes for cooking testicles tend to recommend frying or poaching, although Eliza Acton recommends adding bull's testicles to a curry or a calf's head to add flavour. (Acton, 1845). The general advice for the preparation of testicles is to be careful not to overcook them as they will become hard and rubbery.

How testicles are cooked is very much a matter of national preference. In France they are poached before frying, and in Iceland ram's testicles are preserved in sour whey, whilst in Japan whale testicles are boiled and served with a vinegar sauce. Cock's or capon testicles, known as *rognons blancs* (white kidneys), are prized in France, but the British tend to prefer calf or lamb testicles.

Regardless of what type of testicles are eaten, sensibility runs high and delicacy prevents it being spoken about in clear terms. Writing in *Wine and Food*, No 20, Spring 1939, Ambrose Heath tactfully skirts around the subject of using a lambs testicles in a stew: 'There are a great many parts of an animal that are not ordinarily considered appropriate for the table proper, and are usually eaten by their devotees with a feeling of apology [...]nLamb's tails for example, make an extremely delicious if a little muttony pie, and really delicious stew can be made out of other parts of this small creature the exact nature of which is best kept hid. But these are country joys unknown for the best part, to the townsman.'

If dishes containing testicles were considered best 'kept hid' or at least the exact nature of such dishes' ingredients, then it is perhaps not surprising that recipes containing penis rarely feature in British cuisine. Clarissa Dickson-Wright and Jennifer Paterson – better known as 'The Two Fat Ladies' – ever ready to stray from convention, included a recipe for penis stew which they explain was originally a Jewish recipe from Marcelle Thomal. According to the ladies, the innards, including penis, once played a major role in Jewish cooking.

Their recipe is a simple one that is seasoned with coriander and garlic and aided by a slow cook:

Penis Stew
1 pound of penis, ram's or bull's
3 tbsp oil
1 large chopped onion
2 garlic cloves, peeled and chopped
1 tsp coriander seeds, crushed
1 tsp salt
freshly ground black pepper

Scald the penis, then drain and clean
Place the penis in a saucepan, cover with cold water, and bring to a boil.
Remove any scum, then simmer for 10 minutes.
Drain and slice.
Heat the oil in a large skillet.
Add the onion, garlic, and coriander and fry until the onion is golden.
Add the penis slices and fry on both sides for a few minutes.
Stir in the remaining ingredients with a good grinding of pepper, add enough water to cover, and bring to a boil.
Lower the heat, cover, and simmer for about 2 hours, or until tender.
Add a little water from time to time if necessary to prevent burning.

(Paterson, 1998)

It seems that the sexual organs of animals, while edible, were, because of their symbolic potency and associations, considered by many as unfit for human consumption in modern Western society, and this is especially true of the penis. However, Beijing's infamous penis restaurant embraces the symbolism of the sexual organs of a variety of animals and looks to magnify these qualities.

This rather unusual dining establishment, known as the Guolizhuang Restaurant, is popular with businessmen and tourists alike and is not short of customers willing to spend good money on delicacies like cooked donkey, yak, bull and dog penis, as well as testicles. It is believed that consuming animal genitals increases male potency and does wonders for women's complexion. Certain penis are considered better for different purposes; for example, some dishes are aimed at increasing a man's masculinity and are therefore considered unsuitable for women, whilst a dish described as 'Eight Treasure Grilled Deer Foetus, garnished with broccoli' is purported to be a great skin boost for women. Other curious dishes on the menu include, 'Dragon in the flame of desire', which is a whole yak penis steamed, fried and flambéed, and stewed deer head and sheep's foetus in brown garlic sauce. If you are inclined towards simple dishes then battered bull's penis may be your ideal dish, or if you prefer a fine dining experience an elaborate dish of carpaccio-style deer penis with a spicy wasabi dipping sauce, or dog penis cooked with hot peppers might be just the ticket.

If the idea of eating a chewy, gelatinous and gristly animal penis seems unsavoury then the grim dinner party hosted by Mao Sugiyama in 2012 would be classified as nothing short of abhorrent.

Sugiyama who is asexual, had voluntarily undergone surgery to have his genitalia removed in April 2012. However, in a bizarre move he took his amputated penis and scrotum home from hospital and organised a rather gruesome dinner party for paying guests. Diners were invited to feast upon his severed genitals – which were garnished with mushrooms and parsley – for around £160 each.

In order to advertsise the shocking supper Sugiyama took to Twitter, where he offered to cook his penis for a guest: 'I am offering my male genitals (full penis, testes, scrotum) as a meal for 100,000 yen [£800]. I'm Japanese.' The offering proved popular, with around seventy guests attended the dinner party in the Suginami ward of Tokyo. While five people tucked into Mao Sugiyama's genitalia, the rest of them ate beef or crocodile.

The five lucky diners who opted for the main attraction enjoyed the organ meat cooked by the donor himself, albeit under the supervision of a professional chef. Before tucking into their special dinner, Suginami made his diners sign a waiver agreeing that he could not be held responsible if they became ill after eating his genitalia.

It appears that all the diners survived Suginami's macabre meal, though it is questionable whether any of them would ever find any dish shocking or outrageous after their experience.

Liver

> But I am pigeon-livered, and lack gall
> To make oppression bitter, or ere this
> I should have fatted all the region kites
> With this slave's offal. Bloody, bawdy villain!
> Remorseless, treacherous, lecherous, kindless villain! ...
> For murder, though it have no tongue, will speak
> With most miraculous organ.
> (Shakespeare, *Hamlet* II.ii.554-558, 570-571)

Out of all the organ meats, liver is probably the one most widely consumed today. However, like a lot of offal, it inspires a love or hate reaction. Whilst some people associate a dish of cooked liver with a silky, buttery, melt-in-the-mouth experience, others recoil in horror at the thought of rubbery, slightly granular slabs of punishment.

Liver is cheap and easy to prepare and can be fried or slowly cooked in the oven. Fried with bacon, onions and a mountain of creamy mash is the classic companions, but when the liver is as good as it should be it can be simply served with a hunk of fresh bread and butter. Liver is not confined to that of sheep, pigs, oxen and calves. Livers of all kinds are prepared into pâtés and terrines (pâté is roughly translated from the French to mean something like a paste or coarse mixture), which are a mixture of ground meats, liver and fat to which alcohol and various herbs and spices are added. Enjoyed in fine dining establishments as a starter, with hunks of bread as a good lunch with wine, or at its most basic scraped out of glass jars in the form of liver paste, giving a non-specific meatiness and distinguished by its utter blandness.

At the opposite end of the spectrum is foie gras, the controversial luxury fat liver paste. Foie gras is considered an expensive food product and is made up of duck or goose liver which has been specifically fattened. It is sought after in restaurants and by those with expensive tastes and is often celebrated for its characteristic rich, meaty, buttery taste which differs from traditional liver pâtés. This is achieved by force-feeding.

The force-feeding process is called *gavage* and has been compared to 'torture and cruelty'. The *gavage* technique involves pumping more food than the duck or goose would voluntarily eat down the bird's throat using a funnel fitted with a long tube. The birds' livers, which become engorged from a carbohydrate-rich diet, grow to be more than ten times their normal size, causing them to contract a condition called hepatic steatosis. This frequently results in the birds developing skin lesions, severe tissue damage to the throat muscles and neck wounds which can become infested with maggots.

When the bird's liver weighs 2-3lb (1-1.5kg) the bird is slaughtered for its prized, albeit diseased, liver. Foie gras has a long French culinary history. French chef Jean-Joseph Clause is credited with having created and popularised it in 1779 and was awarded a gift of twenty pistols by King Louis XVI. He obtained a patent for the dish in 1784 and began a business supplying pâté to wealthy clients with a taste for gluttony. However, he wasn't the first person to exploit the way in which waterfowl naturally stock up on extra calories, which they store as fat deposits in their livers and under their skin before long migratory flights. The ancient Egyptians observed the birds gorging on figs and were the first to replicate this natural process by forcing food down the throats of geese, ducks and cranes, an act which is depicted in Egyptian wall-reliefs as far back as 2500 BC. It is unclear whether the ancient Egyptians specifically prized the livers of these force-fattened birds. It seems that the primary motivation for this early *gavage* was the production of animal fat, which the ancient Egyptians used in everything from medicinal remedies to cosmetic preparations. *Gavage* appears to have spread from Egypt to Greece and Homer's *Odyssey* (written around the eighth century BC) contains the earliest written reference to fattened geese, while in the fourth century BC we find the first mention of their livers as a delicacy.

The practice of force-feeding animals for the purpose of fattening them spread from Greece to Rome, where it was readily adopted and adapted. Roman pigs were subjected to having food forced down their throats in the same manner as geese, while tiny dormice were duped into pre-hibernation binges by being kept in total darkness and surrounded by nuts. Not even snails were safe; the Roman cookbook *Apicius* instructs chefs to remove the operculum (the 'little lid' snails use to seal their shells) from live snails before feeding, so the animals will be unable to return to their shells and will swell to unnatural size.

The Roman flair for innovation led to them devising a new merciless approach to force feeding. Having stuffed their living creatures with fruit they introduced honeyed wine to their fig-stuffed geese and pig victims. The resultant moisture and gases expanded the dried fruit in the animals' stomachs, causing a fatal case of dyspepsia. The resultant livers of these animals were termed *iecur ficatum* in Latin, *iecur* meaning liver and *ficatum* meaning figgy.

Modern-day foie gras has sparked much controversy because of its barbaric practices and outright cruelty to animals. It is strange to consider that eating the diseased livers of tormented birds is still considered a delicacy in the twenty-first century. It is not so surprising that people all over the world are currently pushing for bans on the sale of foie gras and that the production of this 'torture in a tin' has been branded so barbaric that it is illegal in the UK (though we are permitted to import, sell, buy, and consume the product).

Concerns over the callous practices employed in force-feeding animals are by no means a new concept. In the first century AD writer Plutarch makes his position clear in a diatribe called 'On the Eating of Meat'. 'For the sake of a little flesh,' he laments, 'we deprive [animals] of sun, of light, of the duration of life to which they are entitled by birth and being [...] Begging for mercy, entreating, seeking justice, each one of them say[s], "I do not ask to be spared in case of necessity; only spare me your arrogance! Kill me to eat, but not to please your palate!"'

After the fall of the Roman Empire the original foie gras, and *gavage*, all but disappeared from European tables under the influence of Medieval Christianity, which ranked gluttony among the deadly sins. However, as rich, expensive and rare food has always been a symbol of decadence and status it is unsurprising that foie gras was re-invented in the eighteenth century.

By the Victorian period foie gras was so popular that machines were developed to help speed up *gavage* feeding and ease the labour intensity of the process. Things have changed, however, and public distaste for foie gras is growing. While it is currently exported to all parts of the world in several forms, it is now increasingly considered inhumane and an archaic, barbaric trade.

Foie gras has enjoyed an enviable popularity, lauded by famous chefs and foodies from around the globe. However, though attempts to create an ethical version have not managed to overtake the traditional production methods, there is light at the end of the funnel. If you're a carnivore you have to accept that very few animals bred for eating will be living peaceably through to retirement, but the introduction of cultured meat, also called clean meat, changes this. Clean meat is the product of cellular agriculture. The process involves using real animal cells to grow meat in a lab, creating a food item that looks, cooks, and tastes like meat, and biologically it is. It comes as no surprise, therefore, that the laboratories have been working on a slaughter-free foie gras, and no doubt ducks and geese will be delighted when it makes it from the lab to the dinner plate.

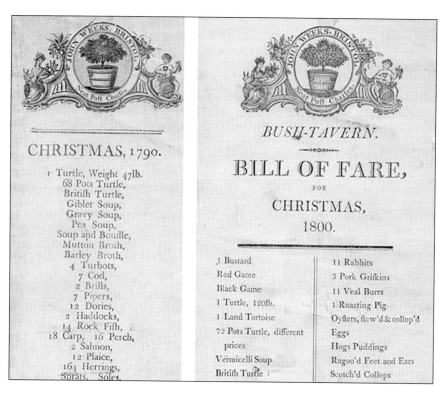

CHRISTMAS, 1790.

1 Turtle, Weight 47lb.
68 Pots Turtle,
Britifh Turtle,
Giblet Soup,
Gravy Soup,
Pea Soup,
Soup and Bouille,
Mutton Broth,
Barley Broth,
4 Turbots,
7 Cod,
2 Brills,
7 Pipers,
12 Dories,
2 Haddocks,
14 Rock Fifh,
18 Carp, 16 Perch,
2 Salmon,
12 Plaice,
164 Herrings,
Sprats, Soles,

BUSH-TAVERN.

BILL OF FARE,

FOR

CHRISTMAS,

1800.

1 Bustard	11 Rabbits
Red Game	3 Pork Grifkins
Black Game	11 Veal Burrs
1 Turtle, 120lb.	1 Roasting Pig
1 Land Tortoise	Oyfters, ftew'd & collop'd
72 Pots Turtle, different	Eggs
prices	Hogs Puddings
Vermicelli Soup	Ragoo'd Feet and Ears
Britifh Turtle	Scotch'd Collops

Above: Bills of Fare from The
Bush Tavern – Christmas 1790
and 1800

Sold £2,400 hammer price:
15 December 2021: lot 279.
(© Dominic Winter Auctioneers)

Right: Welded Cannister Taken
on expedition to the Artic by
Captain William Edward Parry
circa 1826.

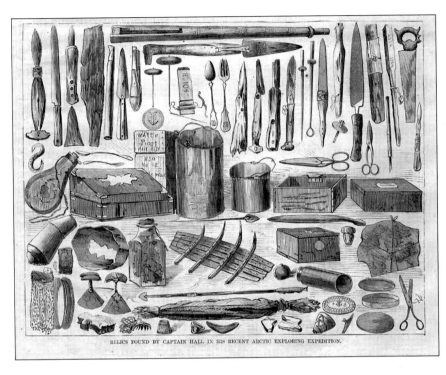

RELICS FOUND BY CAPTAIN HALL IN HIS RECENT ARCTIC EXPLORING EXPEDITION.

Above: Relics Recovered from the Franklin Expedition – 1859.

Left: Example of an Early 19th Century Tinned Food.

Illustration of a Display of Victorian Tinned Goods.

Ductillite

REG. U.S. PAT. OFF.

DUCTILLITE IS THE FIRST REVOLUTIONARY IMPROVEMENT
IN TIN PLATE IN MORE THAN THREE HUNDRED YEARS

● The sardine container is an exacting requirement. The preservation of these delicacies of the deep—billions of them every year, packed in millions of cans—calls for a sound steel of uniform gauge and even distribution of coating.

It is essential that the sardine can be internally pure and externally strong, for safety. It must be made of plate that is light enough and ductile enough for unusual shaping. It must be economical in price and handle easily, with certainty of sealing, in high speed packing.

Tin Plate has furnished the answer to these exacting requirements ... and has done it well.

And now comes Ductillite, made by Wheeling ... the most modern of all tin plate ... bringing lower cost through higher speed in production because Ductillite flows in the dies with minimum breakage and fewer rejections. Ductillite brings also new and deeper shaping for more distinctive packages—and, above all, it carries a base metal with a surface that is more compact, more resistant to corrosion and stain, for the perfect preservation of fish and other foods that are packed in acid juices.

Ductillite is exclusively a development by Wheeling. Its dual contribution of economy and service to the sardine packers is typical of what this modern tin plate means to other branches of industry where quality and low cost are paramount in metal packaging.

WHEELING STEEL CORPORATION, GENERAL OFFICES,
WHEELING, WEST VIRGINIA

DUCTILLITE REFLECTS THE
EXACTING DEMANDS OF THE
SARDINE PACKERS — for the
Unusual in Tin Plate

WHEELING STEEL

Sardine Canning Factory 1935.

British Canning
Machine in Early
1930's.

Grocers' Show Card for
Tinned Peas.

Recipe Booklet from Canned Food Advisory Bureau, London.

Early 20th Century American Tin of Baked Beans with Pork.

Traditional Butchers with Carcasses Displayed outside.

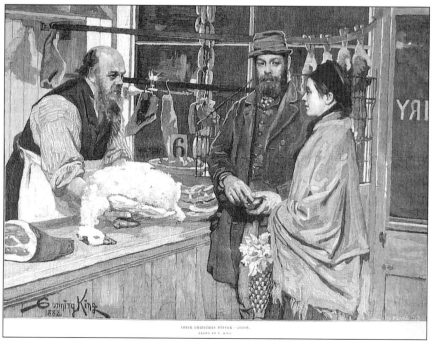

An illustration of a traditional butcher serving a couple to a Christmas goose c1883.

Above left: Game Dealer Weighing Rabbits.

Above right: Plenty of Rabbits – Game Dealer, Mr. Evans weighs his stock of rabbit meat outside Ivor Goodall Butchers, Staveley Road, Wolverhampton.

JS Hill Tripe Dressers – Lancashire.

C 1900 Armours Vigtoral Beef Tea Jar.

Advert for Libby's Food Products with a range including ox tongues, lunch tongues and dried beef c 1900.

Left: Retro Packaging for Frozen Sheep Liver.

Below: Retro Packaging for Frozen Kidneys.

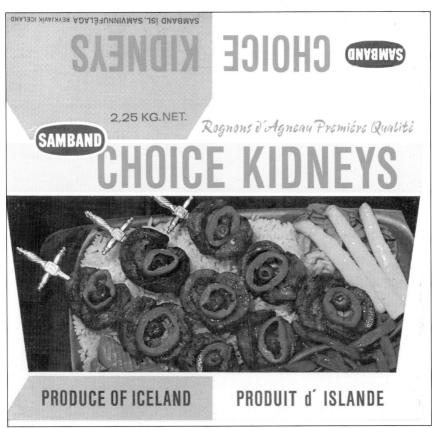

CREAMS OF FOIE GRAS.

MUTTON PIES (OR VEAL AND HAM).

MEATS—Continued	Doz.	Each
TONGUE—CONT'D		
Derby Lamb's in Jelly............10 oz. jars	8 50	75
" Lunch..................10 " "	8 50	75
" ....6 " "	5 60	50
German Ox, Imported........cone shaped tins	....	4 00
Libby's Rolled Ox........No. 1½ "	15 50	1 35
" " " ....2 lb. "	26 00	2 35
" " " ....large jars	20 50	1 80
" " " ....medium "	14 25	1 25
" Lunch...............No. 1 tins	6 10	55
" " ....No. 2 "	13 35	1 20
" " ....½ " "	3 40	32
R. & R. Potted...............3½ oz. "	2 25	20
" " ....6½ " "	4 00	35
Smoked, about 5 lbs................per lb.	....	62
Underwood's Deviled............3 oz. tins	2 65	23
" " ....6 " "	4 10	40
TURKEY		
Brand's Turkey and Ham........10 oz. jars	8 50	75
" " " Tongue........10 " "	8 50	75
Underwood's Deviled.. ....3 " tins	3 35	30
" " ....6 " "	5 00	45

BRAND'S
A·1
PRESERVED FOODS
AND DELICACIES

BRAND & CO. LTD. LONDON—ESTABLISHED 1835

130

Above left: Coloured Lithograph print of Creams of Fois Gras & Mutton Pies from Katharine Mellish's book "COOKERY & DOMESTIC MANAGEMENT". Published in London in 1901.

Above right: Brands A1 Advert for ox tongue and calf's foot jelly.

Right: Advert for Calf's Foot Jelly.

Gordon & Dilworth
CALF'S FOOT JELLIES

This particular form of appetizing nourishment is prescribed by doctors, and used extensively in hospitals, as the most nourishing food for invalids, especially in cases where the stomach will not retain more solid foods.

Patients have thrived upon it, alone, for long periods, with an appreciable gain in strength.

Served with shaved or cracked ice, it will be found tempting to a poor appetite. At a temperature of 60 degrees, it becomes a delicate jelly which will dissolve quickly when placed on the tongue

(In half-pint and pint glass jars, and 9 oz. tumblers)

Flavors: Sherry, Port, Rum and Plain.

prepared by
Gordon & Dilworth
Hammonton, N. J.

102

Left: Cover Design for Varney the Vampire - a series of penny dreadfuls by James Malcolm Rymer, originally published 1845–47.

Below: 1874 – Drinking Blood for Good Health.

Advert for the American Frog Canning Company.

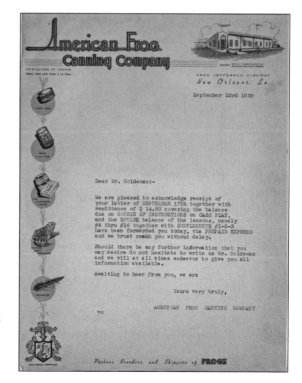

Letter from American Frog Canning Company dated 23rd September 1938 confirming the purchase of a start your own frog business.

Edible insects on a spoon.

Above left: A Vintage Bottle of Cochineal Food Dye.

Above right: Game Birds are traditionally enjoyed 'high'.

Vintage Advertisements for Embassy Stilton Cheese.

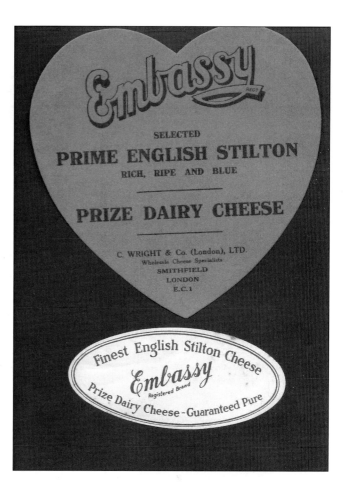

Above left: The Delicacy known as Casu Marzu or 'worm cheese'.

Above right: The Speciality dish known as Balut – a soft boiled fertilised duck egg.

Left: Magic
Lantern Slide of
FISHERMAN
REPAIRING
LOBSTER POTS
C1920.

Below: Illustration
of the meat market,
Paris, during the
siege (1870).

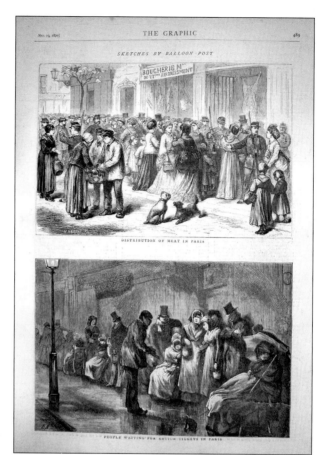

Right: Rat, Cat and Dog Meat for Sale in Paris.

Below: c.1870 people waiting for their meat ration in Paris.

Above left: Illustration of a passenger pigeon c.1833.

Above right: Illustration of Pigeon Pies.

Left: An illustration of Great Auk's.

herbage. It is scarcely raised above the surface, and is mostly wet. The eggs are five or six in number, and their normal colour is white, though they soon become stained with the decaying vegetable matter on which they rest, and before hatching are of a muddy brown hue. The mother bird always covers her eggs with leaves and aquatic algæ before leaving them. The bird has a curious habit of building a kind of supplementary nest, in which it sits until it has completed the structure in which the eggs are to be laid. The young soon take to the water, and are, on their first introduction to the waves, nearly as adroit as their parents.

The food of the Dabchick consists of insects, molluscs, little fish, and the smaller crustaceans.

In its summer plumage the head, neck, and upper portions of the body are dark brown, except the secondaries, which are white. The sides of the face are warm chestnut, and the under surface is greyish white. In the winter the upper part of the body is chocolate-

GREAT AUK.—*Alca impennis.*

brown, and some of the primaries are white; the chin is white, the front of the neck ashen brown, and the under surface greyish white. The total length of the Dabchick rather exceeds nine inches.

The sub-family of the Alcinæ, or Auks, has several British representatives, among which the GREAT AUK is the rarest.

This bird, formerly to be found in several parts of Northern Europe, in Labrador, and very rarely in the British Islands, has not been observed for many years, and is as completely extinct as the Dodo. Almost the last living specimens known were seen in the Orkneys, and were quite familiar to the inhabitants under the name of the King and Queen of the Auks. So agile is (or was) this bird in the water, that Mr. Bullock chased the male for several hours without being able to get within gunshot, although he was in a boat manned by six rowers. After his departure, the bird was shot and sent to the British Museum. The female had been killed just before his arrival.

According to Mr. Lloyd, this bird formerly frequented certain parts of Iceland, a certain locality called the Auk-Skär being celebrated for the number of Auks which nested upon it. The Skär, however, is so difficult of approach on account of the heavy surf which beats upon it, that few persons have the daring to land. In 1813 a number of Auks were taken from the Skär, and, horrible to relate, they were all eaten except one.

The eggs are variable in size, and colour, and markings, some being of a silvery white and others of a yellowish white ground; and the spots and streaks are greatly different in colour and form, some being yellowish brown and purple, others purple and black, and others intense blue and green.

The upper surface of this bird is black, except a patch of pure white round and in front of the eye, and the ends of the secondaries, which are white. The whole of the under

Right: The Great Auk.

Below left: An illustration of a Dodo.

Below right: An illustration of the Ortolan Bunting.

1821.—Dodo, from Bontius.

An illustration of a Rook Shooting Party 1881.

An illustration of rook shooting c.1800.

Above left: Label for Mouse Wine made from mouse pups.

Above right: A Bottle of Snake Wine.

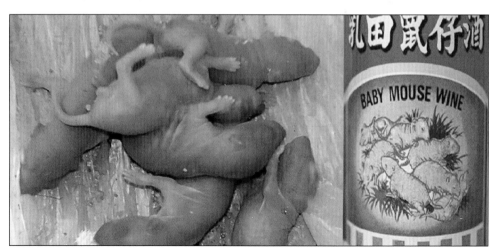

Mouse Pup destined for being made into mouse wine.

Left: Illustration of Rook shooting c 1879.

Below: Illustration of Gipsy cooking around a Campfire c 1886.

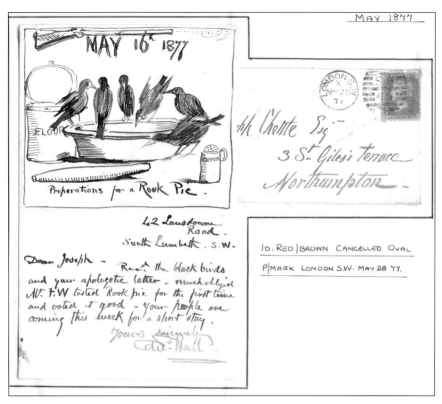

An Drawing of a Rook Pie 1877.

Above left: Game Birds ready for hanging C1890.

Above right: Fishmonger: Mr Pierce of Margate on his rounds c.1935.

Left: Illustration of Oyster Sellers c1863.

Below left: A characterful portrayal of an oyster seller c1880.

Below right: Shuking Oysters C1891.

A REAL NATIVE.

Traditional Fishmongers with crates of shellfish stacked outside and kippers hanging up and proud purveyors standing outside of the Cornish premises.

Chapter 3

Blood Lust

The mention of blood as food may immediately conjure up images of blood-sucking vampires biting into the necks of innocent young virgins sleeping in their beds, but you don't need to be a vampire, real or imagined, to have a taste for blood. Indeed, throughout the ages animal blood has been considered a good source of vitality, containing iron and essential amino acids and even today the concept of consuming blood is not that unusual. Black pudding is considered an essential part of the full English breakfast and consists of pig's blood cooked with oatmeal.

Eating animal blood is a global tradition. Blood puddings (boudin) are made all over Europe and are basically pig's blood and fat. There are regional differences in the making of blood pudding: the Irish use sheep's blood for drisheen, whilst in France onions, chestnuts or small cubes of cooked head meats may be added to their blood pudding, and in Spain they add rice to their blood pudding recipe. Meanwhile in Iceland blood sausages are made during the slaughtering season in the autumn, and their recipe involves the sausages being pickled in whey-barrels.

There are lots of ways in blood is incorporated into recipes, from the Italian sweet dish of sanguinaccio where pig's blood is cooked with milk, sugar, fruit and spices, to boudin à la flamande, the sweet French boudin from the Nord Pas-de-Calais region and which dates back to the late eighteenth century. In this recipe the blood is seasoned with onions, salt, ginger, cloves, pepper, sugar and cinnamon, then finally raisins are added.

The classic coq au vin recipe uses chicken blood to thicken its sauce and so does the British classic jugged hare. There are sweet and savoury recipes for gravies, puddings, cakes, sauces, pressed meats, jellies and custards that all include blood, while the Japanese dry the blood of rattlesnakes to sell as an aphrodisiac. For the Ancient Greeks blood was considered a magical elixir. Pliny the Elder (AD 23-79) described the rush of spectators into arenas to drink the blood of fallen gladiators: 'The blood of gladiators is drunk by epileptics as though it were the draught of life,' he recorded. Centuries later Marsilio Ficino (1433-1499) similarly promoted drinking young blood as a remedy for the elderly to regain their youthful vitality. Anthropophagic remedies persisted for centuries, with medieval executioners fending off sick people who eagerly sought fresh dead bodies to cure the 'falling down' disease.

The thought of blood as a rejuvenating elixir has continued through history alongside our fear of vampires. Elizabeth Bathory, otherwise known as Erzsébet Báthory, gained the nickname the 'Blood Countess' for a supposed litany of crimes against female servants and minor noblewomen who were under her supervision. Bathory was a well-educated aristocrat who was accused of exceptional cruelty to young women. This included whipping with stinging nettles, biting, stabbing, burning of flesh, piercing fingers and lips with iron nails and forcing them to take fatal ice baths. She is even alleged to have smeared a naked girl with honey and left her outside to be feasted upon by ants, wasps, bees and flies. Her alleged depraved acts of cruelty led to her being walled up inside her own castle until her demise, but rumours of her vampirism spread. It has been suggested that she drank the blood of young maidens in order to reduce the effects of aging and many depictions of the countess relate to her bathing in the blood of young nubiles in an attempt to recapture her lost youth.

While the accuracy of these vampire stories is questionable, the concept of youth and immortality being attained through the consumption of young blood is one that has continued even into twenty-first century. The rise in the popularity of the use of blood as an anti-ageing Holy Grail has made the headlines on multiple occasions. The coveted platelet-rich plasma cosmetic procedure, dubbed the 'Vampire Facial', experienced high demand despite its high price tag of around US$1,500. This anti-aging treatment takes a quantity of the patient's own blood, which is then spun in a centrifuge to create platelet-rich plasma and is then reinjected back into the patient's own skin.

On 10 September 2018 *The Sun* newspaper and the *New York Post* published a story carrying the same headline 'Young Blood Could Be the Secret to Long-lasting Health: Study'. The article implied that a published scientific study had made a significant development in the field of medicinal blood drinking, explaining: "Drinking young people's blood could help you live longer and prevent age-related diseases, a study has found. Blood factors taken from younger animals have been found to improve the later-life health of older creatures. The study, published in *Nature*, was conducted by researchers from University College London (UCL), who said it could reduce the chances of developing age-related disorders.' A similar story appeared in *The Sunday Times* in 2017 under the headline 'Blood extract of teenager on sale at just £6,000 a shot'. It reported on how a California company was 'offering $8,000 (£6,200) transfusions of teenage blood claiming that it may provide an array of benefits to older patients.'

In the early 2000s a group of scientists at Stanford University, California, revived a gruesome procedure used in the 1950s known as parabiosis. They paired living mice, young with old, peeled back their skin and stitched together their sides so the two animals shared the same blood circulatory system. A month later the researchers found signs of rejuvenation in the muscles and livers of the old mice. The findings, published in 2005, turned the minds of scientists, entrepreneurs and the public to the potential of using young blood to rejuvenate ageing people. By 2016 interest had grown sufficiently to prompt a Stanford trained doctor, Jesse Karmazin, to found a US-based company called Ambrosia offering infusions of young plasma – the cell-free component of blood – to patients with a median age of 60. It was described by Karmazin as being 'like plastic surgery from the inside out.' According to the company's website, its trial found 'statistically significant improvements in biomarkers related to Alzheimer's disease, cancer, inflammation, and stem cells' after a single treatment. The procedure has come under fire from the US Food and Drug Administration for its lack of proven clinical benefit and for potential safety issues. However, Ambrosia continues to thrive as people search for the secret to eternal youth.

Considering our modern thirst for new blood as a means of joie de vivre then the grotesque imagery of a pale, emaciated consumptive victim drinking blood from a freshly slaughtered cow is somehow more believable or at least relatable. Tuberculosis, or consumption as it was known, has existed for thousands of years and has been a scourge on humanity, cherry picking from the genteel classes and ravaging its way through the lower classes. In 1680 the English writer John Bunyan described it as 'the captain of all these men of death'. Shrouded in myth and mystery, consumption gained an almost cult status in the eighteenth and nineteenth centuries for being a disease that signified good conduct and purity. (Bryder, 1988)

Consumption was a leading cause of death and disability in previously healthy adults in Britain in the 1800s and a huge number of people suffered with it throughout the nineteenth century. The condition drew its name from the way in which it consumed its victims and gradually drained life away from them.

The image of consumption became romanticised in some circles, synonymous with beauty, artistic ability and poetic loss. When it claimed young women, their untimely death was idealised, with descriptions that made their fragile demise appear beautiful: 'suddenly she stopped, clutched her throat, and a wave of crimson blood rushed down

over her breast', wrote Edgar Allan Poe of his wife, Virginia, who was dying of consumption. One of her guests, author Captain Mayne

Reid, describes her as 'a lady angelically beautiful in person and not less beautiful in spirit [...] her grace, her facial beauty, her demeanour, so modest as to be remarkable.' (Quinn, 1998). Even though Virginia was ailing the descriptions of her speak only of how the disease that was killing her served to enhance her beauty: 'And when we talked of her beauty, I well knew that the rose-tint upon her cheek was too bright, too pure to be of Earth. It was consumption's color – that sadly-beautiful light which beckons to an early tomb.' (Silverman, 1991).

The ghostly appearance of youthful women being snatched by consumption was portrayed in virtuous and alluring ways, with the consumptive look becoming fashionable in the eighteenth century. The reality of a disease characterised by the sapping of vitality, diarrhoea and coughing blood was overshadowed by how the frailty of the diseased, with their pallid complexions, dilated eyes and flushed cheeks, was the very essence of aesthetic perfection. As sufferers wasted away, their emancipation was seen as beautiful. Withering was in vogue and the thin, wispy appearances of consumptives were romanticised as being graceful and demure, their fragility the model of Victorian sensibility.

Even though they were nearing death's door consumptive women were depicted as being ideal: the absolute model of femininity. The consumptive look became a desirable one and their quiet, withdrawn demeanour was highly regarded as 'decorous, mild, and meek' were considered the correct way women were required to act and dress. (Day, 2017). It was fashionable to be ill, and while the 'it' girls of the time paraded around sporting their fashionably ill look, the real reason for their frail frames, pale complexions and crimson lips was not spoken of. It became the illness of artists, of those too good for this world. Perhaps by choosing this view of the disease, those left behind could find comfort in the angelic virtues of their beloved lost ones.

Consumption may have been seen as virtuous but it was also feared. It was also known as the 'Great White Plague' or the 'White Death' due to the pale complexion of those affected. It was also given names more befitting of its true ghastliness: 'Robber of Youth', 'Captain of all these men of Death', 'Graveyard Cough', and 'King's-Evil'. The disease was known to strike down all ages, genders and classes of society without discrimination

Feared and revered as the 'white plague' was, it was nevertheless depicted as a decaying beauty that encapsulated delicacy and an enchanting melancholy that appealed to creative souls such as artists and poets. The so-called 'graveyard poetry' was perhaps a vehicle for giving meaning to a disease that was little understood. Lord Byron once remarked to his friend Lord Sligo, 'I should like, I think, to die of consumption.' When Lord Sligo asked why, Byron replied, 'Because then all the women would say "See that poor Byron – how interesting he looks in dying."' (2011)

Emily Brontë described the consumption heroine in Wuthering Heights as 'rather thin, but young and fresh complexioned and her eyes sparkled like diamonds'. Emily died in young adulthood from tuberculosis, along with their mother who was consumed by the illness. In 1819 John Keats in 'Ode to a Nightingale' wrote, 'Youth grows pale, and spectre thin, and dies.' In 1821 Keats, like many others, was claimed by the disease, another helpless victim of the white plague.

Consumption not only inspired the work of creatives but was also credited as being at the root of creativity. *La Dame aux Camélias* by Alexandre Dumas inspired Giuseppe Verdi's *La Traviata*, an opera about a woman with consumption. The protagonist, Violetta, lives an unwholesome, sin-filled life, but achieves redemption through her untimely death.

*****

Consumption wasn't just portrayed as a disease of the righteous, however, it was also one that caused deep anxiety which led to the emergence of gothic tales of vampires and vampirism. The pale, listless and fatigued sufferers of this cruel disease began to be looked upon by some as being the victims of vampires or even of being vampires themselves. By 1800, in New England in the United States, it is recorded that twenty-five percent of deaths were caused by consumption (Bell, 2006) and soon tales began to circulate of vampires being the cause of consumption.

It was common for members of the same family to fall victim to consumption and for members of a deceased consumptive's close family to start suffering symptoms of the disease after their loved one was buried. Rumours began to circulate that the deceased was a vampire who was sucking the life out of their family from beyond the grave and that the symptoms that the deceased displayed before death was actually those of a vampire.

Consumption became linked to vampires through folklore and literary traditions. With no cure available and little effective treatment for the symptoms, people looked to folk remedies and explored extreme 'cures'. There was no knowledge of how consumption or diseases in general were spread and so the sudden illness and death of those who had not shown symptoms until after the death of an anaemic friend, neighbour or relative could be attributed to an attack by a vampire.

Bram Stoker's *Dracula* would not be published until 1897 but folk tales of a ghost or memory of a dead loved one haunting the living and slowly sucking away their energy were well established. The modern idea of this is largely attributed to John Polidori's *The Vampyre* in 1819. Polidori turned the past folkloric monster into a handsome and debonair gentleman, moving through society choosing vulnerable, young and beautiful victims. So the idea that vampires could blend into the everyday lives of the living was born.

The comparisons between the literary portrayal of a vampire and that of a consumptive were strong: their ghostly pale complexion, piercing eyes and blood-smeared mouths provided an intense image. The consumptive became a perfect model for a vampire: they often suffered foul breath due to the rotting state of their lungs and were constantly coughing up of blood; and they were prone to being nocturnal as a result of high temperature spikes at night, making them restless and more active in the hours of darkness.

Cases of 'vampirism' in the United States were taken very seriously, gaining momentum in a similar way to those of the witch trials. One famed incident occurred in 1892 in the small town of Exeter, Rhode Island. George Brown had already lost three members of his close family when his son Edwin fell ill with consumption. Deep in mourning, Brown's neighbours blamed a vampire and suggested that one of his deceased relatives was sucking the life from young Edwin. Upon exhuming the bodies of his deceased family members, his daughter Mercy's body showed no signs of decay and was not in the position in which it had been buried. Fresh blood was found in her heart and she was declared a vampire. Her heart was removed from her chest and burned to ashes, which were then mixed with water and given to Edwin to drink, in the belief that drinking a 'vampire heart' would cure the ailing child. He died shortly after. Not everyone was convinced by the idea of vampires being responsible for deaths, but for some it acted as a convenient explanation for the ravages of this life-draining disease.

Throughout the nineteenth century consumptives in Britain and overseas tried a number of cures. The most popular advice was a good diet and taking fresh air in a warm climate. Adverts for various pills and potions appeared in the press, but these acted as nothing more than a placebo. One advert in 1899 for 'Dr. Williams' Pink Pills for Pale People' proudly announced 'undoubted consumption cured', and went on to explain that consumption was caused by 'having too little blood'. It went on to explain that the pills would ensure you 'make new blood with every dose.' The Pink Pills were widely used across the British Empire, Europe and United States and eventually proved so popular that they were marketed in eighty-two countries. Though these 'magical' pills were purported to cure everything from consumption to cholera, an analysis of them conducted in 1909 for the British Medical Association revealed them to contain sulphate of iron, potassium carbonate, magnesia, powdered liquorice, and sugar. Upon analysis it was discovered that one third of the iron sulphate in the preparation had oxidised and the analysis report concluded that the pills were 'very carelessly prepared'. (British Medical Association, 1909).

With very little help from the medical community and quackery, and superstition being unreliable, people turned their hopes of a cure towards an unlikely source, that of the local abattoir, choosing to adopt the experimental method of drinking the blood of freshly slaughtered animals.

During the mid- to late-nineteenth century, many consumptive victims throughout the United States went to slaughterhouses to drink blood in the hopes that it would cure them; people from all parts of society, men, women, and children. They were never charged money for the blood, and for the most part drank it willingly, barring a few children. Many reported that it did take a few tries to get the first sip down, but after that they would drink about two glasses every visit.

Stories of consumptives drinking blood from freshly killed animals were emblazoned across the newspapers. The *Georgia Weekly Telegraph* ran an article which interviewed a man called, Mr C. H. Stickney who told the reporter he 'drinks half a tumbler of blood twice a day'. An article in the *St. Louis Globe-Democrat* revealed the shocking news that blood-drinking vampires are not just the making of fiction, but actually exist in St. Louis, going on to explain that 'between two and three hundred ... daily drink from a half to a pint of blood, piping hot, from the veins of slaughtered cattle.'

The drinking of animal blood as a 'cure' for consumption or else to boost vitality was by no means unique to the United States. Headlines in Britain also covered the shocking news. In 1874 a report in the *Blythe News* entitled 'Drinking Hot Blood' detailed an engraving bearing the title 'Blood-drinking at the Shambles' in which it describes people consuming animal blood as the 'Paris method of attempting the cure of consumption, which may be regarded as the relic of some superstitious observance'.

An engraving entitled 'Abattoir', published in the 1890 edition of the French journal *Le Monde Illustrè* depicts a group of elegant and seemingly wealthy young women gathered outside an abattoir in order to partake in drinking the fresh blood of a slaughtered cow, in the belief that it would protect them against consumption and boost their general well-being.

Similarly, an engraving in *Frank Leslie's Illustrated Newspaper* from 1894 entitled 'Drinking Beef Blood – Consumptives At The Brighton Abattoir, Boston, Mass' depicts a rather gory scene with a slaughtered animal on the floor, its blood drained and decanted in glasses, two of which are handed to a pair of well-presented young women.

The abhorrence of drinking animal blood is in some respects secondary to the shock of the type of customer this remedy attracted. The *New York World* published an article entitled 'Elegantly Attired Ladies Who Regularly Visit Slaughter Houses'. (*Feeding on Beef Blood*, 1885). In it a lady who arrives by carriage is described as looking to be in 'fragile health' and from the description of her attire she appears to be a fashionable lady of means, 'millions of silk worms had spun away their lives' to make her gown. She hands her coachman a 'large cut-glass goblet' in which to collect the fresh blood from inside the slaughterhouse. The restorative effects of consuming the fresh blood on this particular customer are notable: 'A pretty color had into her whilom, pale cheek, her lack-lustre eyes of a moment ago were sparkling and animated, and as she re-gloved her jeweled hand her gesture and attitude were assured and vigorous.'

While newspapers ran sensational headlines and butchers and slaughterhouses promoted the remedy with great gusto, a more reserved approach was taken by most medical practitioners. Specific mention of the blood cure is brief, if at all, in medical journals and it was certainly not wholly embraced by the medical establishment.

The main piece of medical advice remained 'get outside and get plenty of fresh air'.

Dr William H. Burt's *Therapeutics of Tuberculosis, or Pulmonary Consumption*, published in 1876, explains that 'The use of raw meat, where there is great emaciation, has often been invaluable,' and there is 'no doubt that the blood is really valuable, it being so easily assimilated, but it seems so disgusting we believe but few patients could be induced to use it.'

Those suffering from consumption often had a lack of appetite and found it difficult to eat anything substantial so blood was seen as a rich nutrient that could be taken to help patients build up their strength. While the medical community were somewhat sceptical or else hesitant about prescribing the merits of animal blood consumption it did garner some support in 'Consumption: A Re-Investigation of its Causes' by Dr de Lacy Evans published in 1881. He declared: 'Many people have been greatly benefited by drinking the warm blood of animals. This practice, especially the drinking of lamb's blood, is carried on in many parts of the Continent. Dr Marcet has invented some biscuits, composed of a clot of sheep's or bullock's blood and chocolate; but the blood must be freshly drawn to be of any service. There is no doubt that newly-drawn blood is invigorating, sometimes exciting, and that from it many people have experienced "a great increase of power".'

In Britain the blood-drinking antics of Europe and the United States was watched with a degree of bemusement and understandable scepticism. Preferring to rely upon bottled 'cures'. George Handyside, the author of *Every Man Should Be His Own Doctor,* which sold over a million copies, produced various remedies for everything from rheumatism to alcoholism with one of his most popular cures being for consumption. Handyside's cures were well received and adverts for them appeared in newspapers. One such advert appeared in the *Pateley Bridge & Nidderdale Herald* in 1889. Entitled 'Handyside's Consumption Cure & Blood Purifier, 'it read: 'Consumption Cure,

6d for two bottles, will be sent carriage paid, on receipt of a postal order. The Blood Purifier, - at 2d. per bottle, is nearly as good as the Consumption Cure except where the vitality is very low.' Other remedies, such as Powell's Balsam, had very simple sales messages, 'Coughs Cured And Consumption Prevented' (*North Wilts Herald*, 1880). From Dr Pascoe's Concentrated Cough and Consumption Mixture to Barry's Delicious Invalid Food there were plenty of prettily packaged remedies available, all eagerly vying for the pennies of those looking to recover from or avoid the contraction of consumption.

Headlines of 'Drinking Blood' did sporadically turn up in British newspapers. One such article was featured in the *South London Chronicle* in 1874. It described how the newspaper had 'published a paper by Dr de Pascale recommending fresh blood as a remedy for phthisis and anaemia'. The article went on to explain that the paper had appeared in many journals and that his advice had 'borne fruit in America to an extent that ought to delight him', explaining that in Brighton, Massachusetts 'a hundred patients can be seen in morning at the abattoir taking their turn to swallow a tumbler of the freshly drawn blood'.

In 1879 *The Daily Telegraph* reported in great detail the procedure involved in partaking in the 'unpalatable' drink of blood in France:

> It is not only vampires who drink blood ... for certain maladies, such as affections of the lungs, a general wasting-away of the body, and other diseases, the blood of animals is believed by some to contain special virtues, and to ensure those who drink it almost infallible cure. Whether this belief be fallacious or not, a visit to the slaughterhouse of Villette at Paris, places beyond doubt the fact that it exists, for here, every morning, between the hours of eight and nine, from hundred to a hundred and fifty invalids of both sexes present themselves to claim their mutational glass of blood, which they drain with a

conviction of its beneficial qualities that helps them to overcome the natural repugnance such a draught inspires. The majority of drinkers belong to the female sex, and for the accommodation of these, some whom are maids matrons of high degree, a reception-room is set apart, provided with seats for the patients and their attendants of relatives. The garcon who serves the applicants with the unpalatable beverage has distributed the crimson liquid to the clients for upwards of twenty years, and performs his duties with intelligence which procures him many a pourboire. The nature of the malady from which a person is suffering determines the question whether the blood administered shall be that of cow, sheep, swine, bullock. Each patient is required to bring with him or her a serviette and glass. When all have arrived, the garcon takes the glasses, and returns a few moments after laden with a tray bearing them filled with the nauseous draught, which has to be imbibed hot as the patient can take it. The glasses emptied, fresh ones containing water are offered to the company, who, one can easily understand, are glad to rinse their mouths and purify their palates from the sickly taste of warm blood. They are cautioned, however, to beware of swallowing even the smallest quantity of water, to do so immediately after the draught of blood involving, it is said, imminent risk to the drinker; and to prevent any neglect to this precaution the garcon remains on the watch and promptly snatches the glass of water from the hand of anyone whom perceives in the act of infringing the rule. A glass of animal's blood costs but six sous, so that whether the hopes of the invalid drinkers of effecting a sure cure are realised or not, the treatment is, at all events, not ruinous one to follow.

(*The Daily Telegraph* 'Drinking Blood', 1879)

Although it may seem strange today that people loitered around abattoirs in order to get a drink of warm blood from a freshly slaughtered animal we have a long, global history of consuming animal blood. Blood makes up between three and five per cent of a live animal's weight and whilst the idea of a glass of steaming hot blood might not make it to a list of popular cocktails it is certain that blood is still used in food production and cooking today and is enjoyed by many.

Chapter 4

A Feast of Nymphs Thighs

Mark Twain famously said, 'Eat a live frog first thing in the morning and nothing worse will happen to you the rest of the day.'

The amphibious delicacy of frog's legs is widely appreciated. Indeed, every year the French gobble their way through 4,000 tonnes of frogs' legs. However, that's nothing compared with the huge number being eaten in Asia, South America and the United States. Whilst many people harbour prejudice against eating frogs and others suffer squeamishness at the thought of eating a pond creature and encountering a taste of swamp, it is certain that around the globe frogs' legs are grilled, curried, poached, fried stewed, set in aspic and devoured with great glee and gluttony.

When considering the history of feasting on frogs' legs, the average British diner doesn't spring to mind. No matter how many times someone may wax gastronomical about the 'delicate flavour of the meat' (Montagen, 2001), or that it tastes like chicken, there is a general abhorrence at the thought of eating a pond dweller. A view echoed in *Larousse Gastronomique*, which says frog legs have 'usually filled the British with disgust.'

However, it seems that the British palate may have changed. There are plenty of culinary records that offer proof that the British have a long history of devouring frog flesh. For example, in his seventeenth century cookbook *The Accomplisht Cook*, Robert May included a recipe for a pie made with live frogs that would 'cause much delight' and spur the ladies to 'skip and shreek'.

Even Isabella Beeton included a recipe for 'Frogs, Stewed' in her 1866 *Book of Household Management*. In a report on frog eating in England, the possibility of frog on British tables was explored:

> It is said that frog-eating is likely to become as popular with Englishmen as with Frenchmen. Frog-farming is conducted in the United States on a big scale, and in two years (1895-1896) one farm alone supplied Europe with 500,000lb of skinned forelegs and 700,000 living frogs for scientific purposes. We trust that flesh-eaters who defend their habits on the grounds that by eating animals they cause to be born innumerable creatures that would not otherwise have existed will see the propriety of eating as many frogs as possible, so that farms for their propagation may be established in this country with as little delay as possible.
>
> (*Frog Eating in England*, 1899)

Larousse Gastronomique meanwhile notes that when the esteemed 19th-century chef Georges Auguste Escoffier worked at the Carlton Hotel in London he convinced the Prince of Wales in 1908 to allow frogs' legs at his table by calling them *cuisses de nymphes aurore* (legs of the dawn nymphs). The frogs' legs were skilfully cooked in aromatic stock, carefully dressed with a chaud-froid sauce coloured with paprika, before being decorated with tarragon leaves and covered with chicken jelly. This magical sounding dish was greatly enjoyed and Edward felt compelled to compliment the chef on such a unique and magnificent dish. It is perhaps no surprise that having received the royal socialite's seal of approval, Nymphs' Thighs became the culinary darling of the season. Escoffier's aromatic and cleverly entitled dish was considered a masterpiece despite the fact that the 'thighs' on the menu belonged to imported bullfrogs.

The British tradition of eating frogs' legs, however, may not be attributable to the French. Evidence from a 2013 archeological dig suggests that they may have been an English delicacy 8,000 years before France. Archaeologists digging at the Mesolithic Blick Mead site, close to Stonehenge, discovered the cooked leg of a frog among the charred remains of a feast that is believed to have been prepared around 7,000 BC. Despite the French predilection for *cuisses de grenouille*, a reputation that earned them the derogatory nickname 'Frogs' back in the eighteenth century, it seems that they may not have been the inventors of the dish.

The first records of French amphibian feasts date from the twelfth century AD, when French church records first refer to frogs' legs being eaten. In the middle ages overeating and the consequent weight gain of monks was of concern. Many monks were accustomed to enjoying an abundant and rich diet that was laden with saturated fats resulting in underemployed monks piling on the pounds. Over-indulgence was in clear breach of St Benedict's austere rules laid down around 530 AD, which warned: 'There must be no danger of overeating, so that no monk is overtaken by indigestion, for there is nothing so opposed to Christian life as overeating.' To ensure that monks cut back on their over-indulgent diet and curbed the growth of their waistline, the church authorities are rumoured to have ordered them to abstain from meat on a certain number of days a year. In a shrewd move the monks classified frogs as fish, which didn't count as meat, and so could enjoy many frog flesh feasts. The story unfolds that pious but hungry French peasants duly followed the monks' example and a national delicacy was born.

It is certain that by the seventeenth century frog meat was a popular dish, as evidenced by Alexandre Dumas who, in the 1600s, records in his *Grand Dictionnaire de Cuisine* (posthumously published in 1873) that an Auvergnat named Simon was to be found making 'a most considerable fortune with frogs, sent to him from his region, which he fattened and then sold to the very finest restaurants in Paris, where this foodstuff was very much in fashion'.

Frog meat rose to such popularity over the pond that by 1894 popular reports of large American frog farms were in circulation in Britain. The *South Wales Echo* reported, 'The biggest frog-farm in America is on the backs of Lake Erie, and although the industry is of comparatively recent growth (says *Cassell's Saturday Journal*) frogs to the value of £20,000 to £ 30,000 are annually despatched from this one place, while the aggregate amount spent on this unique table delicacy reaches close upon a quarter of a million pounds sterling.' ('American Frog Farming', 1894). In 1900 one story contained a report explaining that the 'United States Frogman' believed 'that frog- farming is certain to be one of the most profitable industries of many parts of the country, and that already many men are engaged in it.' ('Frog Eating and Frog Farming', 1900).

It seems that the consumption of frogs in Europe and America was increasing during the late Victorian period and that frog farming was expanding to meet this need. The message was clear; money was being made in frog farming. An article in the *Evening Express* in 1902 describes an innovative and profitable industry: 'A new industry is making great strides in Ontario, no less than the culture of frogs – the special kind of edible frog for the French market [...] One frog farm last year produced 5,000lb of dressed frogs' legs [...] The business is said to be so profitable that the Ontario Government is constantly in receipt of applications for leases of lands suitable for frog raising. No doubt we shall soon hear of young Englishmen in want of a Colonial career embarking in this new enterprise.' ('Money in Frog Farming', 1902).

With promises of rich pickings from frog farming and success stories such published in newspapers, interest was building. One such success story was of Miss Mona Seldon, who because of her sight deterioration was forced to retire from teaching and 'began the systematic cultivation of frogs'. The story relayed details of her success: 'her past year's work produced a net revenue of £320. She now has now a steady income from twenty acres of "froggy swamp" of £500 per annum.' ('A Frog Farm', 1896).

In light of the media attention, it is not surprising that the plans to bring frog farming to England were met with a degree of optimism. A report in the *South Wales Echo* in 1888 read:

> If reliance can be placed on a statement made in an American journal, plans are in progress for the establishment of a frog-growing establishment near London, whence these delicacies will be distributed far and near. People who are ignorant of the table value of the edible frog need not be alarmed at this new project (says the London correspondent of the *Glasgow Herald*). The proposed English preserves will take the form of a series of ponds, well planted with vegetable matter, and the frogs will be bred from spawn brought from Austria and France. In winter the animals will be placed in large pits three or four feet in diameter and four or five feet in depth, as in Vienna, where hundreds of thousands are annually stored, being covered with straw in seasons when the weather is very cold. From these receptacles the animals are collected as required. On the Continent a large number of people find remunerative employment in frog- growing, and the business is rapidly extending throughout America, the consumption of that kind of meat in the city of New York being at present about 100,000lb per annum.
>
> ('English Frog Preserves', *South Wales Echo*, 1888)

But while the British were intrigued by frog farms they were not inspired to jump on board the frog farm get-rich-quick scheme.

It seems that frog cuisine and the business of 'get-rich-quick schemes' went hand in hand. As the Great Depression of the 1930s hung in the air like an unspoken truth, the American Frog Canning Company arrived with a pitch for those who were struggling to make a living. The company promised a good market and a steady source of income. Adverts were placed in newspapers and magazines promising, 'good profit – no competition'. Under the bold heading of 'Raise Giant Frogs – we buy what you raise', it is easy to see how people could be lulled into thinking that starting a frog farm in your back yard was a simple way to start a profitable business. After all, the adverts placed in various periodicals, including the May 1936 edition of *Practical Mechanics,* it seemed like very little start-up considerations were required other than 'a small backyard pond of 20 x 25 feet with a little bank space'. And there was the promise of a waiting market. Indeed, the world of frog farming, according to The American Frog Canning Company, seemed an easy business to start up. As the advert said, 'think of the profit possibilities!'

Albert Broel sold a dream of financial stability though frog meat farming. His business model was quite simple; he demonstrated that there was high demand for frog meat and that just one breeding pair of frogs would produce thousands of offspring, meaning that an army of frogs could be established very quickly. At US$5 a dozen, frogs could quickly turn into a fortune. People leapt at the opportunity and thousands applied to Broel for copies of his frog-raising handbook, paid for a full course of frog rearing, and ordered their breeding frogs to start their own farms.

Broel was able to share his knowledge and clearly demonstrate how the system had worked for him. After a failed career in natural medicine he had started growing frogs on a large scale at a 100-acre farm in Ohio as well as experimenting with canning frog meat. This had proved lucrative and in 1933 with the money he made he moved his family to Louisiana in order to expand the business and take advantage of a better climate for frog rearing. Describing frog farming as 'perhaps America's most needed, yet least developed industry,' Broel launched a very successful marketing campaign and essentially started a 1930s frog rush.

Broel's business was two-fold. He ran a successful frog canning business, selling frogs' legs that promised, 'All the goodness of fresh frog legs is sealed in with our special canning process'. He also advertised a product called 'Frog a la Queen', which was described as being, 'pure fresh frog meat blended with mushrooms and other choice ingredients, ready to serve'. The second leg of his business involved the farming of frogs in order to supply his canning activities. He needed a ready supply of frog meat and he could not farm enough himself, and so his idea was to encourage others to grow frogs so that he could acquire a steady supply of frog flesh to meet the demand in his canning business.

Newspapers across America and around the globe detailed the numerous letters they'd received asking for more information about raising frogs, and shared success stories about frog entrepreneurs, from 'society women' in Tennessee to a Japanese frog-raiser in Los Angeles. After Louisiana, Florida had perhaps the next most ambitious frog-farming venture known as Southern Industries Inc., a frog farm located North of Tampa, Florida.

Though no other frog farm attained the success of Broel"s. He was described as 'the nation's largest individual producer of frog legs' by the Central Press. When he wasn't farming frogs, selling the dream of frog farming or writing about frogs, he was creating recipes for Giant Frog Gumbo, American Giant Bullfrog Pie, Barbecued Giant Bullfrog Sandwiches, Giant Bullfrog Omelet, Giant Bullfrog Pineapple Salad, and even Giant Frog Fondue. Indeed, frog meat seemed to be a taste sensation that America just couldn't get enough of. In 'Famous Ways to Serve Giant Frogs' (1934) Bruel wrote, 'Frogs' legs have always ranked first among the most exclusive of food delicacies.'

In a bulletin issued by the Department of Agriculture in 1952 entitled 'Bullfrog Farming and Frogging in Florida', it was explained that 'the value of bullfrogs as a food is now thoroughly recognized throughout the country, and the growth of the industry in the last years attests to the importance of the demand for the giant bull-frogs [...] no article of diet is more sought for.' F.B. Cramer, president of Southern Industries Inc., explained that his frog farm principally shipped 'frog legs as we have two markets that ask for the bodies with legs: Kansas City and St Louis.' (Department of Agriculture, 1954) He continued, ' we could sell every pound we produce at this time to the cannery in Louisiana that specialises in canning frog legs and frog meat.' The American Frog Canning Company was a hungry beast and the demand for its products meant it was always requiring more frog meat.

Frog farming was a real growth industry. It had been documented in the United States from 1900, but the growth of the industry seems to have increased from 1930 onwards. The table below shows the yield of frog meat in weight and US dollars in Louisiana from 1926 onwards.

Year	Weight lb	Value $
1926	44,457	6,668.00
1927	837,735	125,661.00
1928	715,540	107,331.00
1929	984,971	147,746.00
1930	1,044.036	261,009.00
1931	1,856.354	464,089.00
1932	1,206.355	301,589.00
1933	1,817.450	276,618.00

Source: Bulletin issued by the Department of Conservation of State of Louisiana (Department of Conservation of State of Louisiana, 1933).

Bullfrogs were shipped live from Louisiana to many parts of the world including Japan, China and Canada. In 'Bullfrog Farming and Frogging in Florida' it was noted that 'Millions of Louisiana bullfrogs are croaking in Japan today. Frog legs are served at all the leading Japanese restaurants and frog raising in the Orient is becoming an increasingly popular industry.' The world was hungry for frogs, but as the craze continued to grow so too did scepticism about the frog business.

Talking of the frog farming industry, the *Los Angeles Times* wrote that it was 'somewhat ephemeral', while one Midwest paper compared it to rabbit farming, another get-rich-quick scheme meant to harness the reproductive potential of small food animals. The reality was that frog farming was far from a quick business as it took a few years for frogs to grow to a saleable size and in the meantime a lot of feeding and protection was required. Many frog farmers found that their stock died before achieving its optimum size and out of the thousands of start-ups only a few businesses achieved success.

While Broel's canned frog meat was a great success, not even his own successful frog farm in Louisiana could keep up with the demand for raw ingredients, causing him to advertise 'We buy frogs!' in newspapers and on a large sign outside the company headquarters. The truth is that much of the canned frog he sold was actually supplied from hunters who caught hundreds of wild frogs by wading out into the swamps of Louisiana, instead of from the farmed stock he promoted.

Frog hunting grew and became so popular that the state's population of wild frogs was declining rapidly. In his book, Broel used the diminishing supply of wild frogs as a selling point for potential frog farmers, but ultimately it proved the demise of his canning business. By the end of the 1930s Louisiana had passed a law restricting the hunting of frogs in the high season of April-May, resulting in a void that farming could not fill. Broel was forced to shut his canning company down. Demand simply exceeded supply.

The reality of frog farming was a battle against nature and was very different to how Broel's advertisements and other promotions portrayed the opportunities. So different was the frog farming dream that Broel sold from the reality that in the mid-1930s the US Postal Service indicted him for mail fraud. 'Frog Breeders Leap with Cash', one newspaper gleefully reported. Broel and a partner had 'hopped to

New Orleans', as another reporter put it, after cashing in US$15,000 worth of checks for instructional brochures.

One of the most outrageous claims published was that in thirteen years a frog farmer could make US$360 billion growing frogs. Broel denied such as claim. 'I assume it is needless to tell you that I made no such statement,' he stated to one Ohio paper. Asserting that someone else had made the calculation, and it was an illustration he hadn't meant to endorse, it was 'simply published as I publish all other things of interest to people engage in the frog business,' he wrote. 'I think you will agree with me that such a statement is so ridiculous upon its face that it could not seriously influence the judgment of anyone deliberating as to whether or not he should engage in frog raising.'

Undoubtedly people had been swept away by the frog farming hype, but now the frog craze was coming to an end. Southern Industries Inc., the second largest frog farming success, was also facing lawsuits from its investors who had been promised big returns. After one year, they had still received no money, and demanded to know 'why they had received no dividends on their investment in pairs of frogs.' It seems that not even this company's cost-cutting practices of feeding 'the entrails and other parts which cannot be used [...] to the tadpoles', could return quick profits, nor could their diversification into 'tanning frog skins [...] into leather that has already found a good market for making ladies shoes, belts, purses.'

The American frog farming dream went into a deep slumber and while Broel's frog rearing literature with its gory details of shipping live frogs, slaughter pits and catching frogs in the moonlight remains a reminder of the frog farming rush, even the master himself retired from the business.

The demand for frogs' legs, however, did not simply end with the demise of the American farming craze. The global consumption of frogs was seemingly insatiable. In 1910 it was reported that Detroit produced, shipped, and consumed six million saddles of frog (pairs of frogs' legs).

With a taste for frog flesh, Detroit was no safe place to loiter if you were a frog. They were hunted by amateurs and professionals alike. Frogs were speared, poled, 'fished' for using a piece of red flannel as a lure before being hooked and reeled in, or clubbed or cruelly gigged with a pronged fork, the victims often suffering a prolonged agonising death just for the sake of their legs.

The love of frog meat meant that hunting was pursued as a family leisure activity. Lucy Corbett, in her French Detroit cookbook *French Cooking on Old Detroit Since 170*, described hunting for frogs as a child in the 1920s: 'Armed with a tightly covered pail and a sawed in two broomstick to which was fitted a short length of old garden hose, you walked the field. The frogs jumped ahead [...] You socked – whango!' The whole process is described as if a sport rather than the catching and killing of a living creature. Corbett goes on to describe in ghastly detail the skinning process, which included using 'stout shears' to 'take the pants off them.'

It was estimated that a professional frogger could catch around 200 frogs a day, but such catches were unsustainable and as early as 1902 frog hunters were complaining about numbers declining. By 1908 demand exceeded supply and frogs' legs started coming from elsewhere.

The depletion of frogs was so great that in 1913 state representative George Palmer from Detroit introduced the Michigan Bill 404 which was passed into law banning the commercial hunting, sale, storage or serving of edible frogs at hotels, restaurants or public eating places from November to June, thus defining the frog season.

The American love of frogs was remarked upon in 1909 when the US Consul at Marseilles was asked to deliver a report upon the raising and marketing of frogs in France. It was reported that 'he discovered that frogs' are 'not largely or generally used as an article of food'. He quotes a pamphlet by a French authority, who calls attention to the fact that 'a greater demand for French frogs exists in the United States than the markets of New York can supply.' ('Frog Eating New-Yorkers', 1909).

Today the appeal of frog meat is wide. According to a study published in the journal *Conservation Biology*, from 200 million to over one billion wild and farmed frogs are killed every year to meet the international demand for their legs.

Wild frog populations are depleting globally and while regulations have been put in place to protect some of the most endangered species, it is extremely difficult to track which species are being traded. The species most commonly involved in the trade are large-bodied frogs, namely the American bullfrog (*Rana Catesbeiana*), crab-eating frog (*Fejervarya Cancrivora*), and Javan giant frog (*Limnonectes Macrodon*).

Whether you consider frogs' legs to be a few scraps of limp, bland and tasteless flesh or the ultimate gourmet delight, one thing is clear and that is that cruelty and declining numbers is a common theme running through the various methods used to kill frogs destined for the dinner plate. Graphic descriptions of inhumane frog killings have been recurrent through history and still exist today. Grotesque scenes of frogs being skinned alive and having their snouts and rear legs cut off before having their violated torsos tossed into a heap of other bleeding frogs being left to endure a slow, agonizing death doesn't build an appetite.

With the hunger for frog meat seemingly insatiable, frog-rich India and Bangladesh dominated the world trade in frogs for meat. The harvesting of the common Indian bullfrog (*Rana Tigerina*) to meet the Western culinary demand for frogs' legs meant that in the mid-1980s there was widespread concern about the population and welfare of India's frog population. Ecologists were also concerned about the resultant environmental imbalance caused by frog culling: as wild frog populations declined insect populations that the frogs used to control exploded and insecticide usage soared.

The trade in frogs' legs grew exponentially after restaurants in North America and Europe greedily consumed their own native frog populations. Humayun Abdulali of the Bombay Natural History Society noted that the harvest of frogs had increased from 1,500 tonnes in 1963 to more than 10,000 tonnes in 1983. South Asian species were not only abundant but were also popular for culinary purposes because they were plumper.

The animal welfare standards in India, however, left much to be desired. Once caught, the frogs were taken live to cutting rooms where workers dunked them in a salt and chlorine solution to kill bacteria before being butchered. This process was horrifically described by Abdulali: 'The front half of frog resting on its bleeding belly, propped up on its fore feet and staring helplessly at the world around it is a ghastly sight.'

India's frog meat trade peaked in 1981 when 4,368 tons of frog limbs were sent abroad at a value of approximately £20.5 million in today's monetary value. In 1987 the frog trade was banned when it became recognised that there was overexploitation causing ecosystem impacts and animal welfare concerns. However, when India stopped exporting frogs it did not stop the hunger for frog meat and illegal poaching remained a problem.

Amidst concerns over the declining population, a ban on commercial frog harvesting throughout France was initiated, but this did not prevent people harvesting for their own needs. The consumption and consequent demand for frogs' legs has remained despite the harvesting restrictions and has merely moved the source of supply. Markets in both the US and France were initially supplied by native frogs, but these are now satisfied by imported live frogs and frozen frogs' legs from China, Mexico, Taiwan, Ecuador, the Dominican Republic, Brazil and Vietnam, with Indonesia now being the world's largest exporter of frogs, shipping more than 5,000 tons each year. While some of these exported frogs may be farmed it is certain that most of the meat is harvested from the wild.

Frogs legs remain enduringly popular and France still imports the largest number of frogs' legs, closely followed by the US, while Belgium and Luxembourg are also noted connoisseurs. Frogs are to this day still devoured voraciously around the globe.

Chapter 5

Grubs Up

Delicately simmered wasp larvae, preserved ant eggs or some crispy crickets – are you feeling peckish yet? Many people in Western society turn their nose up at the idea of entomophagy (the consumption of insects), but it is a common practice globally and around two billion people regularly eat insects as part of their diet. They are certainly not short of variety in their diet as over 1,900 species are edible. The most commonly eaten insects are beetles, caterpillars, bees, wasps and ants.

We see insects every day, we share our homes with them and they buzz, creep and crawl around us everywhere we go, but for the majority of people the thought of them on a dinner plate is considered outrageously distasteful.

Those in favour of entomophagy explain that insects are of high nutritional value, having a high fat, protein, vitamin, fibre and mineral content that is often comparable to fish or livestock. House crickets, for example, contain on average 205g/kg protein; beef contains 256 g/kg. Termites are also surprisingly protein rich – one species found in Venezuela is 64% protein – while some insects are even as much as 80% protein by weight. Not only are insects protein rich, but they are also rich in essential amino acids and omega-3 fatty acids. Mealworms contain as much unsaturated omega-3 and fatty acids as fish, and even more than beef and pork. Some are also surprisingly high in iron; locusts contain up to 20 mg/100g iron and mopane caterpillars contain a huge 31mg/100g, whereas beef only contains around 6mg/100g.

With such high nutritional merits it is perhaps unsurprising that some people are looking to replace their daily meat with a hearty dish of meal worms. In May 2017 Swiss food safety laws were changed to allow for the sale of food items containing three types of insects, crickets, grasshoppers and mealworms, which are the larval form of the mealworm beetle, making Switzerland the first European country to authorise the sale of insect-based food items for humans. It was in August 2017 that the Coop, Switzerland's second-largest supermarket chain, began selling insect burgers and balls of protein-rich meal worm for human consumption.

As we've become increasingly picky about what we eat, our repugnance at anything other than certain choice cuts from certain animals means that generally things like insects are generally considered disgusting. While research may show that their consumption is extremely sustainable, economical, ethical and nutritious, most people's response is still, 'yuck!'

Insects have a bit of an image problems; they are associated with decay and detritus and thought of as dirty. When it comes to food preparation insects are generally seen as a pest and health hazard not a culinary delight. Indeed, insects plague our picnics and are not considered a welcome part of our daily meal, as an article in 1931 featured in the *Aberdeen Press and Journal* **entitled,** 'Patients "Eating Insects"' demonstrated. The article was reporting on the 'alleged conditions in a Liverpool Hospital'. (*Aberdeen Press and Journal*, 1931) where an infestation of 'millions and millions of ants, steam flies and beetles, blacklocks and crickets, which would disgrace the slums, let alone a hospital' were alleged to have been found. Mrs Caroline Whiteley at Liverpool City Council explained that, 'Jellies, though covered by plates until taken to the table [...] became covered with insects, and sandwiches, instead of being meat sandwiches, became insect sandwiches, the insects eating the meat out of them.'

Let's face it, we look to keep insects out of our kitchens and away from food preparation and so the concept of eating them is an alien one to many people. If a cockroach falls into your prepared meal, even for just a second, it's almost certain that you wouldn't consider eating it. However, insects are not an inherently disgusting food. An estimated 3,000 ethnic groups and eighty per cent of the world's nations eat insects in one form or another and while the Western world's move towards entomophagy may be seen as novelty and a publicity stunt by a few celebrities, eating insects is not a new fad. A British newspaper headline from 1952 read, 'Spiders are a "tasty dish" – "toasted they're grand" says doctor.' The article goes on to explain that 'Dr. W S Bristowe, a naturalist and chemical expert, who ate toasted spiders in Siam, finds them quite a tasty meal, as he will tell members of the Nutritional Society in London.' The purpose of the meeting that took place with the Nutritional Society in London was to discuss 'unusual foods for human consumption'.

But though most headlines surrounding eating insects hone in on the taboo element of the subject a few suggest that we should look to challenge our prejudices around creepy crawlies for tea. *The Independent* in a 2018 article embraced the idea of eating insects and even recommended 'try foraging for, or even farming, your own insects. Every country has a few native insects that can be safely collected and consumed, but only do so in the company of an expert – someone who's eaten them before and lived to tell the tale.' Furthermore, the author went on to explain that 'Humans have relied on a partially insectivorous diet for millennia. We evolved as insect-eaters,' suggesting that because 'Insects are high in lean protein' and were easy to gather than larger prey animals they formed a substantial part of our historic diet and 'may in fact be responsible for our oversized intellect'.

Whilst the thought of dragonfly larvae in a stir-fry or chocolate brownies made with cricket flour may not be everyone's cup of tea, it is certainly not a new concept. In the late nineties the *Sunday Mirror* wrote, 'Toasted creepy-crawlies and barbecued giant spiders are eaten by many Asian and South American tribes,' before suggesting trying out recipes for 'Worm Bread and Beetle Bars'. (*Sunday Mirror*, 1997).

The reality though is that we have been enjoying the culinary delights of insects in our food, drink and confectionary frequently and without revulsion or fuss, albeit unwittingly.

In 2012 a Starbucks barista in the United States noticed that cochineal was listed as an ingredient in the in the company's strawberries and cream frappuccino. Cochineal is made from the *Dactylopias Coccus*, a scale insect that contains a vivid red fluid called cochineal which is a naturally occurring compound. The barista took a photo of the ingredients and shared it with a popular vegan food blogger. The resultant internet publicity storm was reflective of the Western deep-seated abhorrence at the concept of consuming insects. However, cochineal has a long culinary history and its rejection seems to be a modern phenomenon.

For centuries Native Americans used cochineal to colour textiles. Aztecs perfected the art of culturing cochineal insects to be used as a source of dye long before the arrival of the Spanish conquistador Cortés in 1519. Legend has it that Cortés was so impressed by the magnificent hue of the cochineal dye that he took it back to Spain where it became popular in the textile industry. The discovery of cochineal spurred the development of a thriving farming industry to culture cochineal insects and produce red dye. In addition to its traditional use as a dye for fabric, cochineal has a long history as a dye for food, cosmetics and medicines.

The vermillion colour of the cochineal derives from an organic compound known as cariminic acid and it enjoyed great popularity in jellies, icing and baked goods. It was a common ingredient in recipes for Battenberg cake and coconut ice, and there was a time when any recipe that required a shocking shade of crimson or delicate hue of pink would include a dash of cochineal. Was it simply that we didn't know what cochineal was? It seems reasonable to expect that sixteenth- and seventeenth-century Europeans would not have understood widely what cochineal was, although some hypothesised that it might have been a type of worm.

In 1685 when the Dutch microscope pioneer Antoni Van Leeuwenhoek proved that cochineal was actually from a scale insect, he was not dissuaded and neither were consumers. By the late 1700s the knowledge that cochineal was an insect derivative had reached the ears of most educated Europeans and its continued popularity indicates that cochineal was coveted. Far from inspiring revulsion, the use of cochineal in recipes seems to have been on the rise and the liqueur alkermes, which is coloured with cochineal, was enjoying a great reputation as a miracle cure.

Even in the twentieth century people did not appear to be repulsed by the concept of cochineal, and it continued to feature extensively in popular recipes. Cochineal was generally sold as a liquid dye or powder, but even when it was sold in its raw state it looked more like peppercorns than an insect. It was an expensive luxury ingredient, not an everyday staple, and lent beautiful colour to dishes. Those lucky enough to acquire it were unlikely to complain about a dash of insect in their food. It should also be considered that a drop of cochineal was far less unsavoury than mealworms in flour, insect fragments in spices and flies in the butcher's and fishmonger's. Insects were more of a visible part of everyday life than they are today.

By the 1800s sanitation standards were on the up, but this did not result in a decline in the demand for cochineal. Indeed, when faced with a choice between a colouring derived from an insect or the potential harmful effects of artificial red dyes or adulterants such as red lead then cochineal seems a far better choice.

Cochineal did lose popularity, but it was its price that saw this natural colouring fall from grace. In the early twentieth century production of cochineal suffered and artificial red dyes saturated the market. However, after a number of red food dyes were linked to health issues the demand for natural food dyes rose and by the millennium food manufacturers were purchasing cochineal to colour a variety of foods.

Today, cochineal goes by various names on food and cosmetic labels: cochineal, carmine, carminic acid, Natural Red 4, or E120. It is added to sausages and artificial crab to give a pink hue, as well as pink pastries and cakes. It turns up in cheese, sweets and icings. Many yoghurts and juices contain cochineal as well as pill coatings, lipsticks and blushers.

Cochineal was considered an ideal food dye because it remained stable when exposed to heat, light or acidic environments. It also had a long shelf life, had no known safety issues and it blended well, but perhaps most importantly for the home cook was its ability to yield a wide spectrum of shades of reds, pinks, purples and oranges.

Consumer values are changing again and while there is a demand for natural food colourants it seems that it is preferable if these are plant-based as insect based products are either viewed as revolting or they exclude the consumption of those following plant-based diets.

It should be noted that cochineal is not the only insect derivative used in food and cosmetic preparations. *Kerria Lacca*, known as confectioner's glaze or shellac, is made from secretions of the female lac bug. Shellac is used in furniture restoration products and is as a sheen in sweet and tablet coatings as well as in some cosmetic preparations.

While insects are undesirable in many diets and the idea of them ground up in flour or included in taco is rejected in favour of more 'traditional' foods, the fact remains that we may consume insects in a variety of foods without even realising. Insects can lurk in coffee, cereals, grains, chocolate and many other foods and how many insects you consume is dependent to a large extent on the country you dine in. Food supply chains are long and complex so it can be hard for food manufacturers to keep insects at bay.

In the US the Food and Drug Administration (FDA) outlines acceptable limits for the amount of 'insect fragments' allowed in different types of food, including wheat flour, coffee, peanut butter, chocolate and pasta. As much as 10% of food in the US may be adulterated. That is, certain foods may contain insects that are not part of the official ingredient list. For example if a 3.5-oz can of mushrooms contains 19 maggots and 74 mites, it is technically FDA-approved, whereas The FDA legally allows up to 225 insect fragments per 225g of pasta. Indeed, the FDA considers insects 'natural or unavoidable defects in foods for human use that present no health hazard.'

In the UK, things are much stricter, as there are no allowable limits of foreign bodies in food and no published tolerance levels. However, this doesn't mean they don't exist. Field insects, wasps and fruit flies are commonly discovered in fruit and vegetables. Insects that live naturally in fields and orchards may be harvested along with fruit and vegetables and though food companies take steps to remove these insects, some will simply slip through the net. Meanwhile, small grubs are often found in canned vegetables, particularly tomatoes and sweetcorn. Their colour is often cream to greenish brown with long dark and pale bands, but this is variable as is their size (they can be up to 4cm in length). People often think that these grubs may be maggots or caterpillars, but they are moth larvae that live inside the food and are difficult to see during growing and processing. The larvae are killed and sterilised by the canning process so they are not considered a health risk.

It's not just fruit and vegetables that pests are discovered in. White fish such as cod or haddock may be infested with small, round brownish- yellow worms in their flesh. The 'cod worm', known scientifically as *Phocanema Decipiens* are killed through the cooking and freezing process and are considered harmless. The affected parts of the fish are usually cut away but occasionally some may be missed in fresh fish and a worm may be discovered alive. Another parasite to look out for in fish is sea lice, which refers to several species of parasitic copepods that are commonly found on fish in the marine environment. Sea lice have been found in salmon, stickleback, herring and rainbow trout. These usually fall off in harvesting and processing, but a few manage to find their way into our shopping baskets with our intended fish supper.

In addition to insects that hide themselves away in our prepared foods and ingredients there are the food preparation premises that become infested with pests. In the *Belfast Telegraph* in 1972 it was claimed that 'Many people in cafes and food shops were endangering health with their "philosophy of nonviolence" towards pests', explaining that 'Too many people regarded infestation in food premises with a shrug of amusement,' going on to say that 'The London Centre of the Association of Public Health Inspectors said that personnel often worked gaily away in harmony with rats, mice, flies and cockroaches unconsciously providing ideal conditions for their proliferation.' (*Belfast Telegraph*, 1972).

A bakery hit the headlines in 1998 after 'a sliced pan bought by a woman in her local shop was blackened right through with an infestation of flour moth larvae'. The court heard that Modern Bakery, which made the bread, had a bad problem with flour moth larvae. 'A health officer's report stated the bread had been baked with flour "Infested with moth larvae", some of it 11 millimetres in length.' (*Irish Independent*, 1998).

Most cases of infestation result in damaging headlines, fines and the closure of premises, however, not all cases are quite so straightforward. We have recently become a nation of coffee-drinking connoisseurs and while in the United States coffee beans are permitted by the FDA to have an average of 10mg or more animal excrement per pound and much as 4-6 per cent of beans by count are also allowed to be insect-infested or mouldy, in the UK most people don't want to consider sharing their coffee with creepy crawlies. When a couple from Henley-on-Thames discovered a creepy secret in their coffee machine it is not surprising that it made the headlines. In 2018 *The Guardian* reported on how Adrian Turner had an unpleasant discovery when he went to refill the coffee beans in his expensive coffee machine. The article reads: 'He was stunned when bugs began scuttling out. Although he and his wife, Emma, were not familiar with the tiny dark-bodied insects, it emerged later, to their horror, that they were baby cockroaches. These nasty crawlers may be known and unwelcome residents of damp New York kitchens, but they are hardly a common sight in leafy Henley-on-Thames.'

As more and more homes in the UK buy fancy coffee machines, the Turners' cockroach crisis is likely to be repeated across the country. One coffee machine manufacturer has admitted an industry secret: 'We know cockroaches inside of coffee machines is a reality. A disgusting reality. Why do cockroaches love coffee machines so much? They are naturally attracted to three things: darkness, moisture and nutrients. What do coffee machines have? All three. It's no wonder it's a cockroach utopia! With some coffee machines being "fixed", that is, with immovable parts, it may sometimes be impossible to remove everything, wash it down and, perhaps, even fumigate to eradicate the little buggers.' (*The Guardian*, 2018). Such revelations make cricket flour seem quite palatable.

Insects like beetles and weevils may infest dried products such as flour, sugar, milk powder, semolina and pulses if they are stored too long. These insects do not carry disease, but they breed very quickly in warm, humid conditions and spread into uncontaminated food very quickly. And while not everyone may hold with the idea of consuming roasted termites for dinner, the fact remains that whether it is greenfly in lettuce, psocids in the semolina or insects such as beetles and weevils infesting dried products such as flour, sugar or milk powder; insects are part of our daily bread whether we like it or not.

Chapter 6

Debauched Dining

There are many recipes from around the world that are considered decadent by some and appalling by others. From feasts for the wealthy to meals born from desperation and those that sound shocking, improbable or just plain queer, gluttons throughout history have taken great pleasure in dining on dishes that encompass the peculiar and astounding.

It is true to say that there really is no accounting for taste, for what inspires hunger in one person will inspire revulsion and retching in another. From dormice to dodos, if it has breathed we have slaughtered it. Ever-hungry humankind has eaten its way through foetus, beast and curious concoction in its everlasting quest to satiate its hunger for debauched dining.

Some decadents from history have made gluttonous perversion their life's work. Gaius Caesar Germanicus, known as Caligula, was the Roman emperor from 37 to 41 AD. The historical accounts of Caligula and his feasts are somewhat outrageous and are considered in some respects as much a work of fiction as the controversial 1979 biopic which shocked the world with its explicit portrayal of the emperor's brutal and salacious antics. To this day, the highly contentious film remains banned in Canada and Iceland.

What is certain is Caligula is the first emperor to have become notorious for the debauchery of his feasts. Dining at Caligula's table was not for the faint hearted, and while decadence and entertainment was the order of the day, whatever pleasure there was to be had was tainted by the threat of imminent death.

Caligula's reputation was one for cruelty, unpredictability and depravity. The stories surrounding him have built over time and include his incestuous relationships with his sisters and even one where he murdered a sister who was pregnant with his child and ate the foetus. Others tell of how he prostituted his sisters' catamites, stole brides from their very wedding feasts, feeding criminals to wild animals, killing a child for coughing too much, turning his palace into a brothel and committing various acts of cruelty for amusement. Over the centuries a tremendous mythology has grown up around him and many of the things that are popularly believed are simply not true, while others are exaggerated. However, there is undoubtedly some truth in Caligula's sordid reputation.

One the most influential ancient sources about Caligula is a biography of him written by the Roman author Gaius Suetonius Tranquillus (c.69 AD to after c.122 AD), who worked as a secretary to the emperors Trajan and Hadrian. Suetonius was writing in c.121 AD, around eighty years after Caligula's death, and so his accounts are at best based upon hearsay. He is a notoriously unreliable source in part because he has a penchant for telling all kinds of embellished stories about the alleged sexual debaucheries of all the emperors he disliked, including Caligula. His biographies read like gossip columns and he could accurately be labelled a scandalmonger.

So, while any tales of Caligula's dinner parties must be taken with a generous pinch of salt it is certain that they were outrageous and that guests were unlikely to nod off during one. It is said that sometimes he startled his consuls from their feasting by laughing uproariously and seemingly without cause. When they asked why he laughed so, he would reply that it was because he could have them executed at any second. In fact, he liked a good dose of death with his dinner, with prisoners being executed in front of him as he ate.

Caligula's love of spectacle, surprise and luxury was not unusual amongst Roman emperors. Eating was one of the great pleasures of the age and dining with the Roman elite was usually a lavish event: a feast for the eyes as well as the senses. Lust, cruelty, violence and sensuality could also be served daily to the wealthy patricians of

Rome. Food was only limited by imagination and would be served in lavish surroundings in sumptuous vessels such as drinking cups of silver, gold, crystal, agate, amber, and onyx. Finery knew no bounds and Pliny reports that Emperor Nero once paid a million sesterces for a single wine bowl.

As wine flowed and guests gorged on exotic dishes laden with spices and coated with sweet and sour sauces attendants and entertainers saw to their every whim and fancy. As acrobats tumbled and leapt, troupes of naked girls danced under the watchful eye of exotic animals and the music played. Sex, lust and lewdness were served in huge dollops and the wild course of the evening could not be predicted. These meals were devilishly luxuriant affairs that lasted for hours. 'The floor was filthy, muddy with spilt wine, covered with drooping garlands and flowers,' wrote Quintilian of the aftermath of one such feast.

The lust for gluttony meant that vast quantities of food from the sea, field and sky were piled onto the banqueting tables creating an epicure's dream. Guests ate, drank and indulged to excess with the Greek glutton Philoxenus wishing for the throat of a crane or vulture so that he might enjoy his food longer.

Heliogabalus, who was emperor during the western empire's decadent final years, certainly did his best to throw shamelessly lavish feasts. No creature was safe from his appetite. He ordered that the animal kingdom be plundered in order to present the imperial court with an opulent menu of moray innards, flamingo brains, parrots' heads, peacocks and pheasants. He feasted on camel's feet and the combs cut from living birds. Sometimes his feasts would be themed in a particular colour and one occasion he dined for ten consecutive days on the udders and uteruses of wild sows. His insatiable desire for indulgence saw semi-precious stones and pearls served with dishes in a vulgar display of material wealth.

These banquets were all consuming, ravaging resources and elevating the price of food. Indeed, the procurement of food was on a scale of marauding locusts on the warpath. 'The emperor Clodius Albinus would devour more apples at once than a bushel would hold. He would eat 500 figs to his breakfast, 100 peaches, 10 melons, 20 pound weight of grapes, 100 gnat-snappers, and 400 oysters. "Fye upon him (saith Lipsius) God keep such a curse from the earth."' (Walker, 1819).

These banquets were not so much about feeding physiological hunger as being about feeding the hunger for notoriety and status. Generous feasts attested to the great wealth and influence of the host and exotic foods from other countries were highly sought.

While foreign ingredients and animals were showcased other animals that were reared or caught in Rome were fattened, transforming them into a more luxurious dish. Milk was used to fatten snails and dormice, while chewed bread was used to feed up pigeons that were rendered flightless. Birds stuffed with sweet and savoury fillings, live birds stuffed into dead animals, fish of every imaginable type and animal parts from every type of creature were provided in abundance.

The only surviving Roman cookbook is *De Re Coquinaria* ('The Art of Cooking') which is attributed to Marcus Gavius Apiciu. The recipes feature an array of spices and are testimony to the fact that anything that breathed was considered suitable for slaughtering to eat. Pliny the Elder recorded, 'Apicus the most gluttonous gorger of all spendthrifts, established the view that the flamingo's tongue has a specifically fine flavour,' describing him as 'Apicus, that very deepest whirlpool of all our epicures, has informed us that the tongue of the phoenicopterus is of the most exquisite flavour.' (Pliny, 1982).

Pliny's description of Apicus was, it seems, accurate as he ate his way through copious dormice, flamingos, cranes, crustaceans, herons, fish and pretty much anything he could get onto a dinner plate. When he had devoured his fortune he realised that his life of gastronomic decadence was over and so decided to end his life rather than live and eat more modestly.

A lavish diet meant privilege. Elite feasts also served an important political and social function although the theme of these was not always lively. Domitian held a depraved feast with a funereal theme. Against a black backdrop guests were invited to this macabre feast alone, with only their slaves in attendance, and ate by the light of funeral lamps. During this rather ghoulish meal guests were served dishes normally reserved for sacrifices and foods were dyed black by naked slaves painted as phantoms. Only Domitian spoke, and he spoke of death, decay, slaughter and the inevitability of dying. It was undoubtedly a nervous meal and the guests may have wondered whether they were actually attending a last supper. It could have been that this meal was in honour of those who had lost their lives on the campaigns in Dacia or it could have merely been a macabre theme designed to shock.

Domitian was not alone in his desire to create a theatrical funeral feast. Grimod de La Reynière's legendary mock funerary feast of 1783 was a performance which was as much about theatrical trickery as it was about gastronomy. Grimod de la Reynière was a renowned eighteenth-century gourmand, food critic and editor of *Almanach des Gourmands*. He staged his funeral themed meal on 1 February 1783, and not only were guests invited to a funeral procession and burial of a banquet but 300 spectators were also arranged to witness the morbid feast evocative of *danses macabre*. Bringing together the concept of eating and the eaten, Reynière successfully combined his mausoleum masterpiece to combine gastronomy with the Gothic. The event was swathed in black and formed a grim theatrical performance of trickery and ruse, with the centrepiece being a sarcophagus.

Some banquets are not so much themed as a *fête macabre* so much as the food served being reminiscent of the cycle of life through their stark message of death and decay. Plenty of dishes that are still eaten today could be classified as morbid and could tilt the scale of sensibility towards revulsion, though such recipes remain prized as delicacies by those with a sense of gastronomic adventure.

Dishes termed as putrefied are not generally those that stimulate the appetite, yet when it comes to rotten food there is a long global history of eating food in various stages of decay.

Cast aside the urban myth of spices being used in medieval kitchens to mask the taste of bad meat. This tired old misconception has no founding in logical explanation, for there was no need for great medieval kitchens to handle tainted meat and then add expensive spice-laden sauces to such inferior food. While those of limited means may have purchased tainted meat they would not have had any means of dressing it up with spices to disguise its taste. Essentially, if you had the money for spices you had the money for good meat. In Alison Weir's biography of Eleanor of Aquitaine she supposes that 'Stuffings, marinades and rich sauces often flavoured with garlic were used to disguise the taste and smell of rancid meat which had in many cases gone green.' (Weir, 1999). This raises the interesting point about how we used to enjoy eating 'high' meat.

There was a time when game birds were shot and hung, complete with their intestines, until they were matured. Jean Anthelme Brillat-Savarin recorded that, 'Above all feathered game should come the pheasant, but once again few mortal men know how to present it best. A pheasant eaten within a week after its death is more worthless than a pullet, because its real merit comes in its heightening flavor.' The flavour of a matured game birds was preferred and while this might have occurred by virtue of necessity due to lack of refrigeration, there was a penchant for enjoying game birds whose breast meat was aged until green. This trend has changed and people tend not to like their food 'high' anymore. The gamey aromas are considered too close to composition for most modern diners.

The idea of high meat which has been allowed to decompose may seem somewhat unpalatable to today's diner, but the reality is that most meat we buy and consume is decaying, it's just that we use words such as 'matured' to describe the process. Meat is aged to improve its taste and tenderness. As unpleasant as it sounds, the process of aging or maturing meat is essentially carefully controlled decomposition. A freshly slaughtered piece of beef would be tough, but through the ageing process the meat experiences an increase in tenderness and the flavour is altered by a combination of bacteria, enzyme breakdown and oxidation.

There has been a recent trend of eating the 'primal diet'. Dubbed by *The Times* as "the silliest diet ever' in 2009, it consisted of raw meat, eggs and dairy that had begun to decompose. The article went on, 'Hollywood's latest food fad is the most extreme yet.' Julia Llewellyn Smith interviewed a primal diet follower, a 36-year-old man from London, simply identified as John, who explained who told the reporter, 'I'm very keen on a raw hare carcass. Raw mallard is good too. So is raw tongue and raw organ meat. Ideally, it'll have been sitting around for three or four weeks and be really off. Some people like it when it's liquid mush but I prefer it so you can stick a fork in it.' While reports of this diet's effects include slimming, vitality and a radiant complexion, there are also reports of it leaving others ill and explosively incontinent, though fanatics call these side-effects detoxification.

There are a number of reasons why fermented and rotted foods would be important to peoples, whether Palaeolithic or more recent. Fermentation and the more advanced stages of deterioration of meat and fish prior to consumption is the same process that occurs to unfermented food once it is ingested (Zdor, 2003). Fermentation, through the natural post-mortem breakdown of proteins into polypeptides or amino acids, becomes an effective way of preparing foods for easy digestion. In this way meat and fish become softer and more malleable (Fadda et al., Hoz, & Puolanne, 2008). These same processes also contribute to the breakdown, or lipolysis, of fats in the food, liberating a range of nutritionally valuable free fatty acids.

Essentially fermentation and advanced stages of decomposition and putrefaction produce many of the same benefits that cooking does, but without the need for any heating. Fermentation greatly softens the meat and breaks down the component proteins and fats prior to it being ingested. For historically high-protein diets that were characteristic of the northern hemisphere, fermentation and more advanced putrefaction may have offered a more digestible food that required no cooking and required less energy to digest and chew.

Moreover, lactic acid bacteria, which plays a key role in the fermentation process, produce a wide range of enzymes, toxins and other metabolites that inhibit invasion by unwanted pathogens such as *Clostridium Botulinum*, the agent that causes botulism, and others. In regions where drying foods would not have proved efficient and in others where fuel shortages prevented the routine use of fire for cooking fermentation was an ideal food preservation technique. The food was often simply placed for weeks or months in pits in the ground or within specially made seal-skin 'pokes' (Frink and Giordano 2015), or submerged in bogs, rivers or shallow ponds (Fisher 1995). The holes in which the food was buried acted as nature's larder and the fermented foods were retrieved and consumed as required with no ill effects.

Fermented fish heads are still considered a delicacy to older Intuits today. The fish heads are buried in the ground where they are allowed to ferment for weeks before being dug up and eaten as they are. They can be quite soft and almost liquefied, meaning that the eyes and flesh can be sucked clean off the bone. Inuits also catch walrus, whale and seal and bury them in the same way, allowing them to ferment from summer to the following spring when the fermentation process is complete. Kiviaki is a traditional wintertime Inuit food in which whole auk birds are fermented in a seal skin for three month. After fermentation the bird meat is eaten without further preparation. Inuit families in Greenland consider this dish to be festive, and it's often served at celebrations.

Hákarl is a dish of fermented shark meat that is still enjoyed today. Greenland shark meat is toxic when consumed fresh, but after being subjected to fermentation it is safe to consume. The shark meat is butchered and buried for several weeks, after which time it is unearthed and hung to mature. The finished meat is pungent, with the uric acid present in fresh Greenland shark imparting an ammonia-like smell. Hákarl made from the white shark meat is described as having a cheese-like texture, while reddish belly meat is chewier in texture. It is described as tasting fishy or like pungent cheese, but it is generally agreed that the aftertaste can only be described as being that of urine. This could be washed down with Brennivín, an 80° proof schnapps lovingly nicknamed 'Black Death'.

From Sweden comes Surströmming, a fermented food that is better than a strong dose of smelling salts and which is so pungent it's almost always eaten outside. It is an infamous and prized Swedish delicacy made of fermented Baltic sea herring. In spring the spawning fish are caught between Sweden and Finland, then the heads are removed and the bodies are stored in a series of brine solutions. After roughly two months the partially preserved herrings are transferred to airtight tins where they continue to ferment for up to another year.

These soured Baltic herrings could not be sold before the third Thursday in August by royal decree. The mid-20th century ordinance was meant to ensure that all fish underwent a full and proper fermentation process. While this rule is no longer in place the date is still celebrated as the delicacy's premier day. The smell of this food will linger in the air for days and it will cling to everything, including your olfactory memory.

While these techniques are best documented in the northern hemisphere, they have been noted in other regions. The seventeenth-century Dutch colonists observed Khoisan hunter-gatherers (*strandlooper* Bushmen) along the Namibian and South African coast scavenging meat and blubber from stranded whales and storing it in pits along the shore for later use (Smith, 1984), and similar practices have been observed among the Maori of New Zealand. Eating meat in various states of decay was not an unheard of practice in the southern hemisphere. Frank Marlowe notes that the Hadza in

Tanzania were not adverse to making use of rotting meat: 'the Hadza often eat very rotten, week-old meat they scavenge from carnivores.' (Marlow, 2010). After all, we are hunter-gatherers and food would not be passed for the sake of its appearance.

The preservative effects of lactic acid bacteria is instrumental in preventing fats from becoming rancid. This was incredibly important for arctic and subarctic people whose original diets were composed almost entirely of animal foods with high fatty content. Such foods would be difficult to preserve effectively through drying to prevent the lipids, most especially the long-chain polyunsaturated fatty acids, from turning rancid and spoiling. Not only would such spoilage be undesirable in terms of taste but could cause a risk to health. Fermentation provides an effective means of inhibiting the 'autoxidation' of the lipids that leads to rancidity, though such preservation is undoubtedly a creative process, as the Norwegian dish lutefisk clearly demonstrates. Lutefisk is made from dried cod that has been steeped for several days in lye. The finished dish takes on a pale and translucent appearance and has a gelatinous texture and strong aroma.

*****

When it comes to food there is really is no accounting for taste and sensibilities vary hugely. While some may savour bottarga, the dried and salted ovaries of grey mullet or tuna fish, others may turn up their nose up at it. In the same way some would consider the high price of beluga caviar well worth every penny while others would consider a dish of milt, which extracted from tuna's testicles, a more worthwhile investment and rarer gourmet delicacy.

Of course, there are those who would prefer to stick to a simple meal of bread and cheese. In one of George Orwell's more courageous essays, 'In Defence of English Cooking' (1945), he confronts the international consensus about his country's cuisine. He argues that it does have merits and recounts various trips abroad and the British foods he missed while there, which included 'kippers, Yorkshire pudding, Devonshire cream, muffins, and crumpets'. Then there were the English cheeses: 'There are not many of them, but I fancy that Stilton is the best cheese of its type in the world, with Wensleydale not far behind.' Stilton is a classic British cheese and as Robert Benchley, said, 'When all seems lost in England, there is still Stilton, an endless after dinner conversation piece to which England points with pride.'

In thinking about a wonderful wedge of Stilton cheese with a glass of port, maggots don't often factor in one's thoughts, though historically larvae was par for the course. The first literary references made to Stilton cheese were made by William Stukeley in his *Itinerarium Curiosum* of 1722, and later by Daniel Defoe when he visited the village in 1724 and declared, 'We pass'd Stilton, a town famous for cheese, which is called our English Parmesan, and is brought to the table with the mites, or maggots round it, so thick, that they bring a spoon with them for you to eat the mites with, as you do the cheese.'

Another early reference to Stilton cheese is found in a long and rollicking poem written by the Reverend Cuthbert Ellison in 1725 entitled 'Most Pleasant Description of Benwell Village in the County of Northumberland'. Verse CCLXIII of Book I reads: 'Of Pullets young And cold Neats Tongue You shou'd find no great lack, Eke of Green Geese, And Stilton Cheese, Your mouth shou'd keep sweet smack.' The thought of maggots in our cheeseboard proceedings may be more shocking than the reverend gentleman's closing verse:' Thus have You heard From Rev'rend Bard A merry pleasant Farce; If't does not please Ye, Nor makes You easy, Then come, and kiss my [...]'

Today, maggots are not part of the Stilton eating ceremony, so it is possible to keep all of it to yourself. However, according to *The World Cheese Book* edited by Juliet Harbutt, 'The tradition of pouring Port into Stilton came about to kill the creatures that gathered at the bottom of Stilton bells.'

While Stilton may have rid itself of maggots the island of Sardinia had a delicacy called Casu Marzu. Sometimes referred to as 'worm cheese' this cheese it is now illegal to sell, but it is still in demand and it commands high prices on the black market. This traditional Sardinian cheese is started by producing a Pecorino Sardo, a cheese solely made of sheep milk originating from Sardinia. The pecorino is moulded and allowed to sit and cure on a shelf. During this time it gains a nice crust which is then cut off, making it an inviting offer for the *Piophila Casei* fly which is attracted by the cheese, and other dairy products, and lays her eggs in it. The cheese is left in a dark hut for two or three months, during which time the eggs hatch into larvae and promptly begin to eat the now rotting cheese. The excretions that pass through their bodies are essential and are what gives the cheese its distinct soft texture and rich flavour, which is compared to very ripe gorgonzola (which was also traditionally home to maggots).

You may struggle to find this delicacy these days. According to Italian law, Casu Marzu is sell on the market due to the infestation of the *Piophila Casei*. Besides, Casu Marzu is not fully compliant with several provisions in EU food law and legislation. Home making and consumption is not outlawed, just commercial sale, so the cheese remains more than just mythology and is still officially listed as a traditional food product from the autonomous region of Sardinia (Ministero delle politiche agricole alimentari e forestali, 1999).

If you should acquire yourself some Casu Marzu then it is important to make sure the maggots are still alive. Live maggots mean the cheese is in a 'fit and healthy' state and is good to eat. It is rumoured that the more maggots the better the cheese. The other important rule is to avoid looking at your maggots as they can jump up to six inches in the air. The final rule to remember is chew properly! It is essential to chew properly in order to kill the maggots before swallowing this putrid cheese in order to reduce the risk of the maggots burrowing into the intestines. If the maggots manage to survive being eaten the resultant exposure to stomach acid can cause intestinal myiasis, an affliction that causes abdominal pain, fever, vomiting, gastric legions, anal itching, and bloody diarrhoea. There are other risks associated with the cheese. The flies are not only attracted to dairy but to other things including cadavers and therefore pose a risk of contaminating it with harmful bacteria. Also, as the maggots work through the cheese they produce cadaverine and putrescine, compounds that can be toxic in high doses and can trigger allergic reactions. Despite all this, the cheese is also considered to be a powerful aphrodisiac.

It is suggested that Cazu Marzu is best enjoyed with a glass of full-bodied wine, though this could be substituted for a glass of 'mouse wine', especially if you are experiencing a dicky tummy as this drink is a tonic which is classified as a cure-all. In China and Korea mouse wine is made by infusing rice wine with baby mice which are a maximum of three days old. The wine is made by dropping them into a bottle and leaving them to ferment for a year. The finished drink is considered a health tonic that is thought to be a particularly effective remedy for asthma, liver disease and just about anything else.

Baby mice in rice wine may not be everyone's poison of coice, but the attitude towards eating baby animals in general is a complex one. Veal, suckling pigs, spring lambs and game hens are all baby animals and are commonly eaten, but they do attract controversy or revulsion by some. One study conducted in 2018 by psychologists Dr Jared Piazza and Dr Neil McLatchie of Lancaster University and Cecilie Olesen of University College London exposed men and women to images of calves, baby kangaroos, piglets and lambs and measured whether this affected their desire to eat meat. The study recorded that women were more susceptible to finding animals endearing, 'We found that both men and women find baby farmed animals to be cute and vulnerable, and experience feelings of tenderness and warmth towards them [...] Feeling tenderness towards a baby animal appears to be an oppositional force on appetite for meat for many people, especially women.' The images of the baby animals quelled the appetite of diners with strong maternal tendencies, perhaps because young animals display stereotypically 'cute' features that we associate with human infants. This is what ethologist Konrad Lorenz termed *Kindchenschema*, or 'baby schema'.

The sight of young lambs skipping through meadows may put some people off their Sunday roast and leave others reaching for the mint sauce, but when it comes to eating the unborn it is more likely to inspire controversy. Kutti pi is an Anglo-Indian dish consisting of the flesh of an unborn foetus of an animal. It is considered a great delicacy by some, but its availability is contentious dish and while it is legal to sell it, its taboo status means that it tends to be sold from slaughterhouses rather than being available in a general butchers. As kutti pi is not made to order, availability can be limited so acquiring one is just a matter of chance and as consumer demand is high the chance of acquiring one is even less. When cooked the meat is said to be very creamy and soft and is likened to the texture of liver by some.

Another dish that uses the foetus of a sheep, goat or cow is foetal soup. The animal foetus is washed, cut up and added to a stock to make a meat soup. Slink veal comes from an unborn, premature, or stillborn calf and was prized on British tables during the Victorian era, while slink leather (the hide of unborn calves and sometimes lambs) is prized in the fashion industry for bags, gloves and other accessories.

Most cultures eat eggs and a soft boiled egg with toast soldiers is still considered a staple nursery food in Britain, but a popular and common egg dish in the Philippines and Vietnam is Balut, a soft boiled fertilised duck egg that is seasoned with salt and sometimes vinegar and often washed down with beer or brandy. Referred to as the 'Philippine Viagra', these eggs look just like any other soft boiled egg until the shell is peeled back and the small, inert body of a foetal duck, complete with fragile bones, feathers and beak, is revealed. Most accounts suggest that the gooey contents are slurped from the shell with seasoning.

When it comes to eating animals it is not just the consumption of baby animals that causes a mixed reaction, but also the type of animal. While the thought of tucking into a Namibian warthog anus might be considered distasteful, it is rejected for a very different reason to eating a fricassee of Fido. The cultural attitude towards dog meat varies greatly from country to country, but the general consensus is that eating dog meat is strictly taboo.

While serving up a dish of man's best friend is abhorrent to most Westerners, in countries such as Vietnam, China, Thailand and South Korea dog meat is still popular, though some suggest that eating dogs has become less common as pet ownership rises. Taiwan is the first Asian country to outlaw the practice amidst concerns over animal welfare and cruelty.

In countries where it is eaten, dog meat is prepared and cooked in a number of different ways, as with more commonplace meats, but can involve being boiled, skinned or even flash-burned to remove all the fur in one go. The dog meat itself is typically stewed and served with sauce, but canned meat, dog sausages, roasted legs and even dog penis served as a snack is common. Eating dog is not just a culinary practice, but is enshrined in long-standing cultural beliefs about the benefits of its consumption. Ancient folklore associates eating dog meat with luck and good health and some believe it to be excellent for warding off disease and for heightening men's virility and sexual performance.

China is widely attributed with the largest proportion of dog meat consumption and though the trade has been opposed for decades, stomach-churning stories of the whole gory process continue to be printed. Each year in June the city of Yulin in south China holds a festival dedicated to eating the flesh of dogs. *The Independent* reported that 'The Yulin Lychee and Dog Meat festival is an annual ten-day event where over 10,000 dogs are eaten. Cat meat, fresh lychees and liquor are also available at the festival.' (Yulin Meat Festival, 2020). This is a relatively new festival, having started in 2009, though it draws on a well-established tradition, which can be 'traced back at least 400 years'.

The festival at Yulin received a stampede of negative reviews and Dr Peter Li, a consultant for Humane Society International, said that it was a 'bloody spectacle [which] does not reflect the mood or eating habits of the majority of the Chinese people.' However, according to the animal rights organisation People for the Ethical Treatment of Animals (PETA), 'seven times as many dogs die in Bali's dog-meat industry each year as they do in China's Yulin dog-eating festival,' and that dog meat is frequently passed off as chicken.

In the West dogs and cats are considered companions and so while chicken soup might be considered good for the soul, a broth of poodle is considered nothing short of horrific. While considering how certain animals are excluded from the cooking pot on the basis of their companion status, one might consider the plight of the lobster. The poet Gérard de Nerval had a penchant for lobsters, or at least for one lobster, his dear pet, Thibault. In a letter to his childhood friend, Laura LeBeau, after a few days spent in the coastal town of La Rochelle, Nerval wrote: 'and so, dear Laura, upon my regaining the town square I was accosted by the mayor who demanded that I should make a full and frank apology for stealing from the lobster nets. I will not bore you with the rest of the story, but suffice to say that reparations were made, and little Thibault is now here with me in the city.' Having liberated the lobster and saved him from hot water, Nerval was seen out walking his pet on the end of a blue ribbon along the promenade and in the gardens of the Palais-Royal. As word of this eccentricity spread, Nerval was challenged to explain himself. 'And what,' he said, 'could be quite so ridiculous as making a dog, a cat, a gazelle, a lion or any other beast follow one about. I have affection for lobsters. They are tranquil, serious and they know the secrets of the sea.' (The episode is captured by Guillaume Apollinaire in a collection of anecdotes from 1911). Sadly, Nerval ended his life after an emotional struggle with life and poverty. There is no record of what happened to Thibault after his master's death though it is probable to assume that he may have ended up on someone's plate.

Interestingly, during the Siege of Paris (September 1870 to January 1871) the city's populace resorted to eating dogs during. The Prussian forces surrounded France's capital and proceeded to lay siege, cutting off a majority of food shipments. The result was the emergence of a culinary adventure that involved the consumption of nearly every animal in Paris: from camel to rat, dog and elephant. An American doctor, Robert Lowry Sibbet, was trapped in Paris during the siege, describing himself as 'a prisoner in a great city'. He collected his recollections of the time in a 580-page volume, *The Siege of Paris by an American Eye-Witness,* published in 1892. In it he describes how horses were suddenly rounded up for eating before being sent to the abattoir where they were 'blindfolded, struck with a sledgehammer on the forehead and bled with a large knife. The blood is caught in basins and used for the purposes of making puddings.'

France has a long culinary history of eating horse meat. This dates back to the Gaulish Germanic tribes that inhabited the region long before Julius Caesar claimed it for Rome. In fact, the proto-French probably happily ate horse until 732 AD, when Pope Gregory III abolished it as a pagan practice in a move that was suspected to be heavily influenced by a desire to conserve horses for warfare as opposed to reasons of piety. Consuming horse remained technically illegal in France until 1866, although it is certain that horse flesh was consumed before the ban was lifted, especially in the case of peasant horses that became too old to work. While Sibbet himself may have been surprised by the mass slaughter of horses, it is certain that horse would prove to be the high gastronomic point of the siege.

By mid-November rationing was in place and Parisians were restricted to 100g of fresh meat per day. By meat the authorities meant beef, horse and salt fish, but hunger fuelled ingenuity and 12 on November 1870 a stall was erected on the Rue Rochechouart. Sibbet recounted: 'On the right side of the stall was several large dogs, neatly dressed [...] next to these are several large cats, also very neatly dressed [...] On the left of the stall there is a dozen or more of rats stretched upon a tray, and a young woman, half veiled, is timidly approaching them with a little girl at her side. She wishes to inquire the price of the rats, and, if she has money enough, to purchase one,' Sibbet recounted.

Henry Markheim, another chronicler of the siege, summed up these new flavours, 'dog is not a bad substitute for mutton [...] cat, as all the world knows, is often eaten for rabbit.' The rich, on the other hand, 'made merry over their pâtés de rat.' Rat turned out to be pricey. Sibbet recorded that cat and dog meat was anywhere between 20 to 40 cents per pound, but that a 'plump rat' cost 50 cents per pound.

Food was scarce and as prices of all available meat was rising it became a luxury. The price increases of feline meat was remarked upon by the English Politician and writer Henry Labouchère: 'Cats have risen in the market- a good fat one now costs 20 francs. Those that remain are exceedingly wild.' (Labouchère, 1871).

November heralded the closing of most of Paris' famous cafés and restaurants, many being replaced with government canteens where the poor could hope to get something to eat. For Christmas dinner Sibbet notes that he had 'roasted horse meat, a small dish of potatoes, excellent wheat-bread and plenty of wine,' while spending a guilty thought for the working-class Parisians standing in line for thin horse-bone soup.

One of the establishments that remained open was the much celebrated Restaurant Voisin on Rue St Honoré. In peacetime it was frequented by the rich and famous including the Prince of Wales. The renowned chef Alexandre Choron decided to serve up a memorable Christmas midnight feast, entitled "99TH DAY OF THE SIEGE'. This menu was essentially a walk around the zoo with choices that included stuffed head of donkey with sardines and radishes, elephant consommé, bear shanks in pepper sauce, 'cat with rat', and camel roasted, English fashion.

As wealthy gourmands eyed up exotic meat, there was little that was safe from the glint of the knife and fork. Cellar rats, yak and zebra were all devoured gluttonously. Labouchère remarked: 'All the animals in the zoological gardens have been killed except the monkeys; they are kept alive from a vague and Darwinian notion that they are our relatives, or at least relatives of some of the members of the government, to whom, in the matter of beauty, nature has been bountiful.'

The meat of exotic animals was sold through specialist butchers, which was as much about commercial necessity as it was about upholding reputation and not allowing the eating of exotic meats as being associated with desperation and hunger (Rebecca L. Spang, 2002). Not everyone's could afford to dine on elephant and so in such instances animals previously considered pests or pets were turned to. But even these were a privilege, as Labouchère, says: 'This morning I had salmis of rats – it was excellent – something between frog and rabbit. I breakfasted with the correspondents of two of your contemporaries. One of them after a certain amount of hesitation allowed me to help him to a leg of rat; after eating it he was as anxious as a terrier for more.' Though it seems that rat was popular and commanded a good price, the Parisians could not bring themselves to admit that they were reduced to consuming such a dish or indeed serving it. Labouchère continues, 'I was curious to see whether the proprietor of the restaurant would boldly call rat, rat on my bill. His heart failed him – it figures as a salmis of game.'

Nathan Sheppard, an American who kept a journal throughout the Paris siege, attended a dinner consisting of titbits and luxuries including 'Jugged cat with mushroom,' 'Roast donkey and potatoes,' 'Rats, peas, and celery,' and 'Mice on toast.' 'It would be difficult to take a restaurant meal now in Paris without being served one of the animals,' he concluded. (Nathan Sheppard, 1871).

When considering cooking rat, *Larousse Gastrononomique* advises that the best rats are to be found in wine cellars, perhaps because they rats spend their lives steeped in the stuff. Indeed, when considering a recipe for rats one needs to look no further than this excellent resource:

Entrecote à la Bordelaise
Skin and de-gut your rat. Rub with a thick sauce of olive oil and crushed shallots. Add salt and pepper. Make a fire from broken wine barrels. Grill the prepared carcass over it.

It is recommended that the rat be served with a traditional Bordelaise sauce.

Adolphe Michel, editor of *Le Siècle*, attended a dinner where 'dog cutlets with petits pois' and 'brochettes of dog liver' appeared on the menu. The dog cutlets were not prepared to his taste but the brochettes were 'tender and completely agreeable.' (Michel, 1871). Cat meat is described as having an 'agreeable appearance,' though Labouchère struggles with his own sentimentality when eating dog: 'I own for my part have a guilty feeling when I eat dog. I had a slice of a spaniel the other day, it was by no means bad, something like lamb, but I felt like a cannibal. Epicures in dog flesh tell me that poodle is by far the best and recommend me to avoid bulldog.' Though no such sentiment was felt when consuming elephant: 'I had a slice of Pollux for dinner. Pollux and his brother Castor are two elephants, which have been killed. It was tough, coarse, and oily, and I do not recommend English families to eat elephant.'

One poem scrawled on a butcher's cart declared that Paris would never be beaten by hunger. Once all the horses are gone, it would 'eat its rats, cats, and dogs.' (Michel, 1871) and they truly did.

The eating of these animals highlights how crisis, food shortage and war can change human-animal relations and how pets and vermin can suddenly change status to become reconsidered as food. Labouchère, though he struggled eating dog himself, was confident that the siege 'will destroy many illusions, and among them the prejudice which has prevented many animals being used as food'.

There was certainly no shortage of recipes for cooking dog in the 1870s and dozens of culinary books for dog meat were published in France. However, I suspect that the Western world today remains more inclined towards cooking for our dogs and cats than towards cooking with them.

Chapter 7

Eaten to Death

Gluttony is one of the seven deadly sins listed by Pope Gregory I around the 600 AD, but throughout history humans have greedily devoured everything they can and this can be clearly demonstrated in the foods we have eaten. There are some foods that we have found so delectable that we have gorged ourselves on them and eaten them to extinction. Though we may not have found these foods revolting, our shameless destruction of these species surely is.

When the Ancient Greek philosopher Theophrastus wrote of a wild orchid called satyrion which, when dried and ground to a powder, formed the basis of a drink which allowed a man to perform seventy acts of intercourse in a row, little could he have known that he had written the death warrant of this plant. Excitable males all over Greece seized upon it, to the point that it was eaten to extinction. But it would not be the only victim of human excess.

There have been many foods that we have eaten to their extinction including the dodo, the passenger pigeon, Stellar's sea cow and the great auk. The song of these ghost foods still echo, but we don't seem to hear it and our willingness to eat other animals out of existence continues.

Passenger pigeons were the most populous bird in the world during the eighteenth and nineteenth centuries. John James Audubon, the French-American naturalist, attempted to survey and document in drawings all the native bird species of North America in the course of his studies in 1833. He identified the passenger pigeon, *Ectopistes migratorius,* as the most abundant bird on the continent. Indeed, there were reports of flocks extending to a mile wide and 300 miles long and taking 14 hours to fly overhead. In Audubon's research he recorded a mile-wide flock of migrating pigeons that passed over his head and blocked the sun for three straight days.

Joel Greenberg explains that in 1854 strange clouds were reported in Ohio, the origin of which were discovered to be pigeons: 'As time went on it became clear that those clouds were birds,' says Greenberg. 'And as more time passed, they were plunged into darkness. People who had never seen the phenomenon before fell to their knees in prayer, thinking the end times had come. The down-beating of hundreds of millions of wings created drafts. People were cold.'

The passenger pigeon's demise was a dramatic one. It was clearly a prevalent species yet by 1900 only one solitary pigeon remained. The last passenger pigeon was named Martha, after Martha Washington, wife of former president George Washington, and she lived her life in solitude in Cincinnati Zoo until finally in 1914 her death rendered her species extinct.

While Martha's life was considered precious, achieving avian celebrity status, the lives of her ancestors had been considered very cheap. Passenger pigeons were slaughtered en masse and they were the cheapest source of protein around.

Congregating, breeding and migrating in very large groups, they were easily slaughtered in their hundreds of thousands and sold as meat. They could be culled in great numbers with hunters communicating by telegraph to locate large flocks and dispatch them by barrel. Soon the clouds of pigeons were baked in pies adorned with their feet, and their feathers and wings were also used for a number of common purposes. (Passenger Pigeon, 1915).

Pastry topped, stewed, potted, fried or roasted, the passenger pigeon was a staple for many North Americans and was rarely off the menu. An article published in Michigan in 1843 reported:

Pigeons – warm weather has brot [sic] innumerable quantities of pigeons. The air is filled with them, and in the morning so densely that they darkened the sun. A continual firing of guns is kept up, and a graceless scamp was heard singing the following:

"When I shoot my rifle clear,
to pigeons in the skies,
I'll bid farewell to pork and beans,
And live on good pot pies."

(Pigeons, 1843)

Recipes appeared in popular cookbooks and in newspapers. Mary Lincoln includes recipes for braised pigeons, pigeons stuffed with parsley, potted pigeon and roasted pigeon in her popular *Mrs. Lincoln's Boston Cook Book*. Similarly, pigeon features in Rorer's *Philadelphia Cook Book*, published in 1886. The most popular way of eating these was undoubtedly in a pie, though today you would have to manage with a faux passenger pigeon pot pie: 'To make a pot-pie, line the bake-kettle with a good pie-crust; lay in your birds, with a little butter on the breast of each, and a little pepper shaken over them, and pour in a tea-cupful of water — do not fill your pan too full; lay in a crust, about half an inch thick, cover your lid with hot embers and put a few below. Keep your bake-kettle turned carefully, adding more hot coals on the top, till the crust is cooked. This makes a very savoury dish for a family.' (Mitchell, 1935).

A year after Martha had fallen of her perch for the very last time a newspaper headline in Washing D.C read: '$10,000 reward for two fresh eggs.' ('$10,000 Reward for Two Fresh Eggs', 1915). The article explained that, 'The wood or passenger pigeons were the commonest of all birds in the early days of our land, and were to be found all over the country. They were to be sure, killed by millions, and as in the case of the buffalo, there was wanton destruction [...] In a little over a decade they were finally exterminated. The feature went on to give details of the reason for the reward: 'The government's anxiety to find these nests is that the authorities hope to breed these wood pigeons once more.' The reasoning for doing so was not culinary but that of ecological balance: 'For they are the one kind of bird that may be depended upon to keep down the moth pests that are now fast [...] laying waste to our farms.' Needless to say that not even a large reward could lead to the discovery of any passenger pigeons.

Though countless animals have been rendered extinct, the dodo has remained an enduring symbol of loss. When talking about extinction, the dodo's name is inevitably the one that will come up, perhaps because this curious, flightless bird captured our imagination; from Lewis Carroll's *Alice in Wonderland* to David Quammen's *The Song of the Dodo* the memory of this creature has been elevated to that of mythical beast.

The image of the dodo as a clumsy, fat sitting duck, an oddity of nature that lacked the intelligence and agility to avoid the cooking pot of hungry sailors who landed on the isolated island of Mauritius at the end of the sixteenth century is neither a complete nor accurate tale. Often portrayed as a comical animal, the dodo belongs to the pigeon family. Over the course of millions of years of evolution it is thought to have developed into a large bird and lost its ability to fly. The first published record of the bird dates to 1599, a year after the Dutch claimed Mauritius, turning the island into a port of call and, later, a settlement. Sometime during the second half of the seventeenth century the last dodo gave up the ghost.

Many studies have been conducted into the rise and fall of the dodo and it has been suggested by several of them that these birds were much quicker, leaner and upright than some of the depictions we hold dear (Leon P.A.M, 2015). Such depictions were often based upon bad taxidermy exhibits.

Though the Dutch sailors and settlers did eat the dodo it is unlikely that this alone caused its extinction. This was likely to have been caused indirectly by introducing a variety of non-native species, including pigs, goats, deer, monkeys and rats to the island. As dodos were flightless birds, their nests were an easy target for predators. Some of these creatures, particularly pigs and rats, would have eaten dodo eggs and chicks, while others competed for food. As dodos only bore one egg a year the destruction of chicks and eggs would have been catastrophic to their long-term survival as a species.

While we may mourn the loss of the dodo its extinction came long before scientists were willing to accept that species really could vanish forever. Why, they argued, would an all-powerful God consign some of his valuable creations to such a fate? They simply expected that somehow, somewhere, there would be more of these creatures. The French palaeontologist Georges Cuvier is widely credited with making the scientific world aware of the reality of extinction, though this was not until 1796.

Even once we became aware of the concept of extinction our behaviour did not change, as the great auk could have testified if any had survived hunting by mankind. Great auks were flightless birds that were killed for their valuable feathers, pelts, meat and oil by hunters and collectors. Its fate had been predicted as far back as 1785 by explorer George Cartwright. 'A boat came in from Funk Island laden with birds, chiefly penguins [Great Auks],' wrote Cartwright, 'But it has been customary of late years, for several crews of men to live all summer on that island, for the sole purpose of killing birds for the sake of their feathers, the destruction which they have made is incredible. If a stop is not soon put to that practice, the whole breed will be diminished to almost nothing.'

Sometimes referred to as the 'original penguin' – its scientific name was *Pinguinus impennis* – the great auk lent its name to today's penguins, which were named due to their resemblance, though they are biologically unrelated.

Great auks had been an abundant species that lived and bred in harmony in Iceland, Greenland, and northern Scotland until the mid-sixteenth century when European sailors began to explore the seas and harvested the birds and their eggs in great numbers, condemning the species to a doomed future.

The sad fate of great auk lay in the fact that it was worth more dead than it was alive. In 1534 French explorer Jacques Cartier wrote, 'in less than half an hour we filled two boats full of them, as if they had been stones, so that besides them which we did not eat fresh, every ship did powder and salt five or six barrels full of them.' Likewise, in 1622 Captain Richard Whitbourne said sailors harvested the auks 'by hundreds at a time as if God had made the innocence of so poor a creature to become such an admirable instrument for the sustentation of Man.'

The great auk was wanted for more than its meat. Sailors coveted the oil rendered from the bird's fat, while pillow-makers prized its down. Having exhausting the supply of eider duck feathers in 1760, feather companies sent crews to great auk nesting grounds on Funk Island. The birds were harvested in vast numbers each spring until, by 1810, no more were left on the island. It is no surprise that the great auk disappeared from Funk Island as an account by Aaron Thomas of HMS *Boston* from 1794 described how the bird had been cruelly and shamelessly slaughtered until its inevitable demise:

> If you come for their Feathers you do not give yourself the trouble of killing them, but lay hold of one and pluck the best of the Feathers. You then turn the poor Penguin adrift, with his skin half naked and torn off, to perish at his leasure. This is not a very humane method but it is the common practize. While you abide on this island you are in the constant practice of horrid cruelties for you not only skin them Alive, but you burn them Alive also to cook their Bodies with. You take a kettle with you into which you put a Penguin or two, you kindle a fire under it, and this fire is absolutely made of the unfortunate Penguins themselves. Their bodies being oily soon produce a Flame; there is no wood on the island.
>
> (Fuller, 1999)

By the 1770s the island of St John's in Canada had outlawed feather and egg collecting and imposed a public flogging penalty. In 1775 the Nova Scotian government asked the Parliament of Great Britain to ban the killing of auks, presenting a petition. The petition was granted and anyone caught killing the auks for feathers or taking their eggs was flogged. However, fishermen were still allowed to kill the auks if their meat was used as bait, and the consequent scarcity of the birds made them even more valuable.

In 1840 Lachlan McKinnon and four other men were hunting seabirds on the cliffs of Stac an Armin on St Kilda. They happened upon a great auk sleeping on the cliff and having a mind to make profit they captured it, tying it up and taking it to their bothy. Unsurprisingly, the bird was startled and made a lot of noise and fuss. At the same time a storm was gathering and the men became spooked by the uncanny sounds of the bird and came to believe that it was a storm-governing witch. Only three days after capturing the auk, they beat it to death:

> It was Malcolm M'Donald who actually laid hold of the bird, and held it by the neck with his two hands, till others came up and tied its legs. It used to make a great noise, like that made by a gannet, but much louder, when shutting its mouth. It opened its mouth when any one came near it. It nearly cut the rope with its bill. A storm arose, and that, together with the size of the bird and the noise it made, caused them to think it was a witch. *It was killed on the third day after it* was caught, and M'Kinnon declares they were beating it for an hour with two large stones before it was dead: he was the most frightened of all the men, and advised the killing of it.
>
> (J.A Harvie- Brown, 1888)

The lifeless body of the last great auk to live in Britain was thrown behind the fishermen's bothy. The accounts of the killing on Stac an Armin is based mostly on the somewhat unreliable recollections of Lachlan Mackinnon in interviews that were given nearly half a century after the event. Some recent research by John Love has raised the possibility that the long-accepted date for the St Kilda incident is wrong, suggesting that this event did not take place in 1840 but actually took place eight years later, in 1848. If Love is correct then Lachlan and his gang might have dispatched the last ever great auk in the world.

In 1844 sailors found a pair of breeding great auks on Eldey island off the coast of Iceland. These birds were strangled and during the murderous struggle one of the men crushed the egg the pair were incubating and so the last breeding attempt of this curious bird was extinguished.

Whether the great auk of St Kilda was the last one in the world or whether the members of a small fishing expedition of 1844 killed the last ones is perhaps immaterial: the fact is that this bird was hunted to extinction and was lost forever due to human greed.

It took less than thirty years for the Steller's sea cow to become extinct, its downfall due to the fact that this peaceful herbivore was found to be tasty. Steller's sea cow was first seen by Europeans in eighteenth century around the Commander Islands in the Bering Sea between Alaska and Russia.

Georg Steller, the German explorer who discovered the creatures in 1741, noted that these amazing creatures breathed air, never submerged, and may have walked on land. Instead of teeth, the fork-tailed creatures munched on sea grass and kelp with an upper lip of white bristles and two keratin mouth plates. They were monogamous, social, and mourned their dead. The few accounts of the Steller's sea cow come from the sketchy records made by Steller and sadly they mainly record the killing of the creatures that would swiftly see them extinct: 'When a female was caught the male, after trying with all his strength, but in vain, to free his captured mate, would follow her quite to the shore, even though we struck him many blows,' described an explorer hunting the sea cows in 1751. 'When we came the next day, early in the morning, to cut up the flesh and take it home, we found the male still waiting near his mate.'

Steller and his crew hunted the animals for meat, but the sea cows were also an indirect victim of the European fashion industry. There was a great demand for fur and seal skin and as fur traders made their way from Russia and China across to North America they would slaughter Steller's sea cows as a source of fresh meat for their hunting expedition. By 1768 the sea cow had been eaten to death.

*****

The saying, 'you can't teach an old dog new tricks' seems to be very true of humans, for despite having eaten many species to extinction, we seem to be determined to continue allowing our hunger to be a destructive force to other species.

Meet the Ortolan, a delicate song bird that is at the centre of a gastronomic ritual that is so morally questionable it must be performed behind the veil of a large napkin. The ortolan is a small bird with a clear and pretty song. Each bird weighs less than an ounce and is so tiny that eating them could be considered pointless, yet they are considered a great delicacy and are consumed whole in a monstrous scene of messy bone crunching.

The species has been listed as protected under the European Commission's Birds Directive since 1979, but continued to be hunted. Indeed, the killing and selling of ortolans has only been banned in France since the late 1990s, though the ban was not strictly enforced until 2007. The government at the time decided to act after unregulated hunters were catching huge numbers to supply restaurants and the bird's decline was becoming evident. France's League for the Protection of Birds claimed that ortolan numbers plunged by thirty per cent in the decade between 1997 and 2007. Meanwhile, European population updates in 2016 found their numbers had dropped by eighty-eight per cent since 1980. (Jiguet & & Selstam, 2016).

The rarity of the ortolan is only part of the reason why killing and eating it is so controversial. The method in which these songbirds are caught and killed really conveys the gluttonous obscenity of this dish.

Poachers catch the birds using traps set in fields during their migratory season. The netted birds are then kept in covered cages, encouraging them to gorge on grain and figs in order to double their size. It is said that Roman emperors stabbed out ortolans' eyes in order to make them think it was night and encouraging them to feed. The ortolan spends its last days on earth gorging in the darkness before being plunged, alive, into a vat of Armagnac to drown.

Eating an ortolan is a gory spectacle. While the dish may be considered a high point in gastronomic experience, it is an expensive and exclusive dish, and the eating of them is unrefined and messy, a primitive ritual that represents shameless gluttony.

Ortolans are cooked for eight minutes and served whole, complete with bones, innards and with their heads still attached. The shame-hiding napkin is draped over the diner's head; tradition dictates that this is to shield the sight of such a decadent and disgraceful act from God's eyes. Though some suggest that it is to help keep the aromas of the songbird in, thus heightening the sensory effect of the dish, it is certain that the napkin is essential to maintain the dignity of the diner and protect fellow diners from a grisly spectacle.

The tradition is said to have originated with the famed French epicurean, lawyer and writer Jean Anthelme Brillat-Savarin, who once said, 'Tell me what you eat, and I will tell you what you are.' In 1890 Queen Victoria dined on them at Waddleston Manor, alongside dishes such as jellied trout and quail stuffed with truffles and foie gras, and sweet soufflés decorated with gold leaf. The tiny songbirds were a dish that former French President Francois Mitterrand included at his gluttonous last meal in 1995, in which it is alleged that he feasted upon two of the controversial birds.

The napkin-draped diners pick up the whole hot bird by the head and place it feet-first into their mouths, saving only the beak. Connoisseurs of this dish say that the combined crunch of the fragile bones, meat, fat, and the rich flavours of organ meat make for a hedonistic culinary experience. Indeed, the late chef Anthony Bourdain described eating ortolan as a 'sort of a hot rush of fat, guts, bones, blood and meat [...] really delicious.'

Jeremy Clarkson ate an ortolan during his *Meet the Neighbours* series in 2002, in which he travelled around Europe. He raved about the flavour of the dish saying, 'It's really good. It is fantastic, fantastic,' before a uttering a customary witticism over probable viewer complaints. There is no doubt that ortolans are a divisive dish; some romanticise over it as being a wondrous, ancient flavour and part of a long tradition, whilst others see it as barbaric.

While ortolan hunting is banned, the bird is far from safe. There is a lucrative black market and French hunters in the south have continually sought exemption to regulations, arguing that their catches are a small fraction of the bird's broader population. Meanwhile a host of prominent chefs have argued that this is a cultural gastronomic tradition dating back to Roman times that should be allowed to be fulfilled. Human hunger, it seems, continues to be prized above all other considerations, even when the food concerned is really a morsel no larger than a baby's fist.

Similarly, ambelopulia is Cypriot 'delicacy' made of pickled, roasted or poached blackcap warblers and other songbirds illegally trapped in their thousands in Cyprus each year. The tiny birds are eaten whole, legs, bones, innards and all. There is high local demand for these traditional but illegal 'delicacies'. This market is the financial driving force behind what has become a mass annual slaughter of migratory birds, most of which come from mainland Europe. In the past ambelopoulia was a food for the poor, stemming from a time when a few birds were taken for the family table and helped eke out the family rations. However, the dish has evolved into an expensive whim that has nothing to do with sustenance. Today, ambelopulia represents a coveted taste of the forbidden and is usually eaten in secrecy.

Illegally trapping of these birds has become a multi-million pound black-market trade in which mist nets and lime sticks are used to catch blackcaps and song thrushes as well as any other unfortunate birds that fly into the traps. Fake birdsong is used to lure the birds to their sad ending. Each autumn millions of songbirds fly south from Britain and Europe to winter in Africa. They concentrate along migration routes but around the Mediterranean an estimated 25 million are killed by poachers

Nearly half of the migratory bird species from Europe, Africa and the Middle East are thought to stop to rest on Cape Pyla. The most recent figures from the conservation group Bird-Life Cyprus estimate that almost 900,000 were killed here over the course of one year.

This lucrative poaching business carries the risk of fines and imprisonment, but the average fine is €400 and only a handful of people have gone to prison, so in reality the lucrative and tax-free earnings that are available outweigh the risks for poachers. Indeed, the trade in songbirds for the table is so huge that it is thought to be worth around €15 million a year. This tradition has certainly grown over the years and has now taken on a ritualistic element.

It is worth mentioning that, historically, small birds, including song birds, were widely consumed until around the seventeenth century in Britain. In accounts of medieval banquets, 'small byrdes' are frequently listed, with finches, larks, wagtails, warblers, thrushes, starlings and blackbirds all featured on the menu. Pierre Blot, in *A Handbook of Practical Cookery* (1867), gives a list of birds eaten in the French repertoire which includes robins, blackbirds, lapwing, meadow lark, plover, thrush, 'and other small birds'. Isbella Beeton features recipes for roast ortolan, rook and lark, while in Francatelli's *Plain Cookery Book for the Working Classes* (1861), he recommends

'A Pudding made of Small Birds', suggesting, 'industrious and intelligent boys who live in the country, are mostly well up in the cunning art of catching small birds at odd times during the winter months'. Wild birds did fade from popularity in Britain, but the practice was still commonplace in the 1950s and gradually faded with changes in taste, sentiments and legislation.

*****

Shark fins have been regarded as a prized delicacy for centuries, and despite being cruel and threatening endangered shark species they remain firmly on the menu and have become increasingly popular with wealthy diners.

The process of finning is nothing short of barbaric. It involves slicing fins off live sharks and tossing the wounded animals overboard, where they sink to the bottom of the sea to await a painful and undignified death. Unable to swim and pass water over their gills they suffocate, die of blood loss, or get eaten by other predators.

The fins are boiled before the skin and meat is scraped off them, leaving behind the prized softened protein fibre, which is added to the soup.

Shark fin Soup is considered a luxury dish in Asian countries, notably China, where its use can be traced back to an emperor from the Song Dynasty (960-1279) who is thought to have invented the dish to display his vast wealth. Shark fin eventually became exalted as one of the four treasures of Chinese cuisine, along with abalone, sea cucumber, and fish maw (swim bladders).

Abalone is relished in restaurants in China and elsewhere in Asia and the insatiable appetite for this sea snail has seen wild populations crash in the twenty-first century due to over-harvesting. Though these strange and fascinating sea creatures have been prized as a delicacy in Asia for centuries, they were an expensive and rare treat that only the financially privileged could afford. However, by the

1980s the demand for sea snails suddenly grew alongside the growth of the middle class in China as more people could afford to dine on expensive and exclusive foods. Today, they're typically served in expensive restaurants or sold as specialty ingredients and dried and packaged in ornate boxes. The lucrative trade of harvesting the abalone is threatening several species of sea snail that are popular for culinary use.

Beluga sturgeon are now mainly associated with the expensive caviar that commands thousands of pounds per kilo. However, this large and ancient fish is a victim of fine dining and cocktail parties and overfishing them for caviar and flesh has had a devastating effect on their population. Caviar is the hallmark of fine dining; the jewel in a canapés crown and one that remains synonymous with dinner jackets and cocktail dresses. Classified as the ultimate food of the rich and refined, caviar has a very unrefined secret. Until just a few decades ago fishermen would haul beluga sturgeon out of the Caspian and Black seas and extract the caviar in the traditional 'Russian fashion' by cutting out the roe sacks that held their eggs before throwing the fish back into the sea as waste. As a result of the high demand for caviar and the savage harvesting technique, sturgeon became critically endangered. The international trade in wild sturgeon from the region has been banned since 2006, and although there are a growing number of sturgeon farms around the world that attempt to make the process more sustainable, the methods used to extract the eggs, and the morality of dedicating valuable resources toward producing this symbol of luxury, mean the ethics of caviar remain questionable. The future of the sturgeon remains uncertain and while some complain that farmed caviar has a muddy flavour that cannot rival the clean taste of 'real' wild caviar it is certain that connoisseurs must accept that only gluttony and indeed the gluttonous can be blamed.

Lessons have certainly not been learned from history as there are endangered animals today that symbolise humans' willingness to eat creatures out of existence. According to Professor David Macdonald of the University of Oxford, our culinary habits back in 2016 threatened 301 land mammal species alone with extinction

The eighteenth-century social philosopher and economist Bernard Mandeville, who authored *The Fable of the Bees*, put forward the idea that society needs luxury goods to drive consumption and growth through envy and status, expressing in many respects the original 'greed is good' sentiment. However, greed and aspiration seem to have a very high cost and lead to many losses in the natural world, especially when the greed is of a culinary nature.

Chapter 8

What's your Poison?

Taste is subjective and when it comes to our choice of drink it is said that the choice tipple can speak volumes about a person. While a choice of wine, lager or spirit may reveal things about a person's class, career or personality, what do drinks that are mouldy, macabre or outright rotten say about their creators and drinkers?

There is a certain feeling of revulsion that is reserved for occasions when a whiff of something that is 'off' or 'not quite right'. An unpleasant smell can be enough to churn the stomach of those with the strongest of constitutions. While the sight of furry fungus creeping over food is nauseating to most, fungus and bacteria-ridden ingredients are vital to some highly sought after drinks. Cast aside thoughts of pleasant smelling fermenting yeasts, which are a fungus after all; no, we are instead referring to things that are rotten.

In Japan the tradition of mouldy drinks go back over a thousand years. The brewing of rice-based sake is considered a time-honoured art and at the centre of the process is koji, otherwise known as the fungus *Aspergillus Oryzae*. It is impossible to imagine Japanese cuisine without soy sauce, miso, or the rice-based spirit known as sake, but all of these well-loved culinary delights depend on the fungus koji which enables their creation through fermentation.

In a bizarre practice, koji spores are sprinkled onto damp rice, which is left to fester until white fungal 'candy-floss' becomes visible. This is then fermented with water and yeast to make a rather potent brew. The enzymes produced during this process break down the rice starches into sugars. These sugars are in turn fermented to produce up to twenty-four per cent ethanol ABV within the short time-frame of twenty days. The process is rather amazing though the exact history behind what possessed the Japanese to begin experimenting with mouldy rice is unclear. It is possible to get a nasty case of food poisoning from eating rice that has been left hanging around at room temperature or has been reheated. Uncooked rice often contains spores of *Bacillus Cereus*, a bacteria strand that is capable of reproducing prolifically and can cause food poisoning. This bacteria can survive when rice is left standing at room temperature and is reheated; the spores can grow into bacteria, which will multiply and can produce toxins that cause vomiting or diarrhoea.

Consuming mould is something that generally has implications to health and well-being. A prime example would be that of ergot, a fungus that when ingested produces a long and terrifying list of symptoms which include itching, spasm, seizures, numbness, nausea, vomiting, diarrhoea and swelling. In addition to all of the other symptoms it can restrict the blood vessels in the fingers and toes causing dry gangrene. One of the most striking side-effects of ergot poisoning was its ability to cause psychosis and hallucinations.

It has been suggested that ergot-tainted rye may have been the root cause of accusations of witchcraft at the Salem witch trials. The trials began in the spring of 1692 after two girls in Salem were reported hallucinating, experiencing fits, making strange sounds and contorting themselves. Similar experiences were recorded among six other girls and malevolence was thought to be the cause. A total of 150 people were accused of witchcraft in the subsequent trials, various explanations have been offered and one such explanation involved ergot poisoning.

In the 1970s Linnda Caporael, a graduate student at the University of California at Santa Barbara, presented the theory that these 'bewitched' girls were acting this way because they ingested the fungus ergot. The muscle spasms, psychosis, double visions, nausea and sweating would have all been consistent with ergotism. In a paper published in 1976 Caporael stated that 'Assuming that the content of the court records is basically an honest account of the deponents' experiences, the evidence suggests that convulsive ergotism, a disorder resulting from the ingestion of grain contaminated with ergot, may have initiated the witchcraft delusion.' (Caporael, 1976).

Ergot thrives in warm, damp climates and Caporeal argued in her paper that the weather conditions in the area during the year before the witch trials started would have been favourable to the fungus' growth.

It is certain that ergotism has been recorded throughout history and ergot poisoning has even been put forward as a theory to explain the mysterious and inexplicable abandonment of the *Mary Celeste*.

Early Koji experiments may have been a case of trial and error, perhaps kill or cure. While *Aspergillus Oryzae* is safe for human consumption its close relative *Aspergillus Flavus* produces harmful aflatoxins that can cause acute liver disease and can prove fatal. In 2003, 120 people were reported dead after eating mouldy corn that was affected by this poison.

The use of *Aspergillus Oryzae* in commercial food and drink production seems to be limited to Asia, but there are plenty of fungal and bacterial tipples around the globe.

When thinking about the British classic ginger beer it's hard not to think of the landmark case of the decomposing snail in the ginger bottle that saw a shell-shocked Mrs Donoghue emblazoned across the papers. On 26 August 1928 she visited Well Meadow café in Scotland with a friend who ordered her a bottle of ginger beer. During the course of enjoying her drink, Mrs Donohue discovered the decomposed remains of a snail, which couldn't be seen in the bottle until most of it had been drunk.

As a result May Donohue was taken ill and diagnosed as suffering from shock and severe gastroenteritis. She proceeded to sue the manufacturer, Mr Stevenson. The case was a landmark in consumer law, but dead snails and landmark legal cases aside, ginger beer has a mouldy secret.

While the phrase 'lashings of ginger beer' did not actually appear in the Famous Five, the sentiment was surely there. There is nothing quite like the zesty zing of real ginger beer in glorious summer weather. The original ginger beer, however, is nothing like the carbonated drink that is sold in bottles and cans today. 'Real' ginger beer is made from a 'ginger beer plant', which is a nice-sounding term for a symbiotic colony of bacteria and yeast (SCOBY), which resembles a gelatinous, semi-opaque layer of slime. When placed in water with sugar and ginger it produces a drink that is naturally fizzy, slightly alcoholic and very refreshing due to the presence of *Lactobacillus Hilgardii* bacteria which gives it a tang.

The history of the ginger beer plant is murky and there is no definitive answer as to how it ended up fermenting on windowsills around Britain. One theory is that it was brought back by British soldiers fighting in the Crimea; SCOBYs such as kefir and kombucha are popular in parts of Russia.

As can be seen in the recipe for a ginger beer plant below, it grows with each 'feeding' and as a result the SCOBY was often divided, or bits of it that separated were given away to friends, family and neighbours. This process in turn allowed it in time to accumulate an increasingly complex miscellany of microbes. In the late nineteenth century Harry Marshall Ward studied a selection of ginger beer plants and discovered around a dozen different micro-organisms that were all happily rubbing together. The ginger beer plant, like koji, is harmless to humans and can be enjoyed without risk, as long as you look out for sneaky snails lurking in the bottom of bottles.

GINGER BEER PLANT

To start the plant: put 2oz yeast in a large jar (a 2lb jam jar will do). Add half a pint lukewarm water, two level teaspoonfuls sugar and two level teaspoonfuls ground ginger. Leave overnight. Next day add to the jar one teaspoonful sugar and one teaspoonful ground ginger. Repeat this for the next six days. On the eighth day strain off the liquid and put in a basin. Add to it two cups sugar dissolved in two cups boiling water, 12 cups cold water and the juice of two lemons. Bottle and keep for seven days before using. There will be a sponge-like substance left in the original jar. Steep this in cold water for 1 ½ hours, drain, divide in two and start again with half the plant instead of the yeast.

(*Belfast Telegraph*, 29 October, 1980)

While the ginger beer plant is the stuff of happy picnics, fellow SCOBY kombucha is not quite as harmless and though risks are generally considered low, it has been linked to cases of nausea, vomiting, allergic reactions, aches and pains, jaundice and even death.

The 'Noble Rot' or *Botrytis Cinera* is a type of fungus that shrivels and decays wine grapes and in some circumstances can be a winemaker's dream. The sight of luscious grapes shrivelling under the veil of decay can be a very welcome sight and a cause for a celebratory drink.

'Noble Rot' is a type of *Ascomycota* within the funghi kingdom. Other *ascomycetes* include the antibiotic penicillin, Stilton blue cheese and the fungus responsible for athlete's foot. *Botrytis Cinerea* is common and attacks around 200 plant species, including fruits, vegetables and flowers. It is the same greyish mould with a fluffy appearance that can blanket neglected fruit. While this mould can wreak havoc in a vineyard in some circumstances, it can also be a blessing; this is all down to timing. If the mould strikes at the end of the growing season when the fruit is overripe, it will grow slowly over the surface of the fruit without attacking the tissue of the fruit, this is because the fruit has already begun to shrivel, dehydrate and the sugars have become concentrated. The fungus helps to remove further moisture from the decaying fruit while concentrating sugar levels and creating glycerol. The results are a richer, sweeter wine with distinctive flavour.

Sommeliers use terms such as 'honey', 'beeswax' and 'ginger' to describe the flavours that *Botrytis* imparts to wine. This could be because Noble Rot wines often have higher levels of a special aroma compound called phenylacetaldehyde.

Sadly a bowl of strawberries wearing a fur coat will not make for good home-made wine, it is a job that only overripe dehydrated grapes are qualified for.

When it comes to fermenting drinks seagull wine is rather an acquired taste. Made by placing a dead seagull into a bottle of water and allowing it to ferment in the sun, this drink is a dubious choice but has been traditionally enjoyed by Inuits.

On a hot summer day a glass of cider may seem like the ideal drink to relax with, but there is a well circulated story that old cider makers added a rat to the cider vat to aid fermentation, though many say this is just myth. A 1902 feature that was published in the *St James Gazette* suggests that rats were a great addition to the strength of cider making. In the article entitled 'Rats in the Cider Vat', the article laments the lack of attention given to improvements in the art of making cider and how such developments have consequently been carried out haphazardly, giving rise to many a tale: 'Hence arose many stories of accidental improvement – some of them true and others mere intentions. In one well-authenticated and recent case a Sussex vat acted as a sort of rat-trap, every rodent that attempted cross the lid dropping in to meet death by drowning. As may well conceived, this increased the alcoholic strength enormously, and what had happened finally became known through the fact of labourers being found so frequently drunk near the cider-vat, to which they bad found surreptitious access.'

No doubt rodents made their way into cider vats and cider-makers may have felt that rats and mice did little harm in the cellar during fermenting time. After all, an old tradition was to add a piece of raw meat or the remains of the Sunday joint to the vat, for the simple reason that the protein feeds the yeast and restarts fermentation.

Though it is not just rodents that have committed suicide in a bath of cider, there is a tale of a pig disappearing during the cider-making season. The pig was considered stolen, but it was noted that the cider that year was exceptionally good. Only when the large cider vat was empty revealing the bones of the pig at the bottom did the whereabouts of the pig become clear and the improved quality of the cider become apparent. Rough cider is highly corrosive because of its high acidity and after the pig had toppled into the vat and drowned the cider had completely dissolved the meat off the its bones.

If rotting or mouldy drinks are not really your cup of tea and cider with rat or porker are not appealing, then you could wet your whistle with a stout that is infused with bull testicles. The Wyncoop Brewing Co makes an infamous brew called the Rocky Mountain Oyster Stout which is an artisan-brewed stout made with 25lb of sliced and roasted bull testicles. This apocryphal drink started out as an April Fool's joke, but the concept proved popular and the drink is now classified by the company as 'world famous' and is described as 'an assertive, viscous stout with [...] a luscious mouthfeel and deep flavors of chocolate, espresso and nuts.'

Roasted testicles may seem rather a bizarre ingredient for a stout, but back in 2015 The Choice Bros brewery in Wellington, New Zealand developed a stag semen 'Milked' Stout for The Green Man Pub in the city. The brew, which was the brainchild of The Green Pub owner Steve Drummond, contained a rather controversial ingredient, a measure of 'export quality' deer semen that was supplied by a local stud farm. The same pub also offered an apple-infused horse semen shot that apparently proved popular.

When it comes to curious drinks recipes Iceland are clear leaders with their dung-smoked whale testicle beer. Stedji microbrewery in Iceland smokes whale testicles with sheep dung to produce its seasonal Hvalur 2 brew, which was first unveiled in 2015 and sold out almost immediately. It has proven a popular seasonal tipple ever since. If testicles cured with dung sounds palatable then it is worth considering that the brewery uses fin whales, classified as endangered on The International Union for Conservation of Nature's Red List of Threatened Species.

There is cocktail that is a must for anyone with a foot fetish, or more specifically a toe fetish. Established in 1973, the 'sourtoe cocktail' has become legendary in Dawson City in Yukon. Containing a real human toe that has been cured in salt, it is a unique and surreal concept.

The first toe is rumoured to have belonged to a miner and rum runner named Louie Liken, who had his frostbitten appendage amputated in the 1920s. Legend has it that Liken preserved it in alcohol as a memento. In 1973 Yukon local captain Dick Stevenson discovered the preserved toe while cleaning a cabin. Seeing the item as rather a novelty he took it to the Sourdough Saloon and proceeded to dunk it into the drinks of those who were plucky enough to rise to the challenge, and so the Sourtoe Cocktail Club was formed.

Sadly, Liken's toe was not destined for longevity as, according to the Sourtoe Cocktail Club, 'in July 1980, a miner named Garry Younger was trying for the sourtoe record. On his thirteenth glass of Sourtoe champagne, his chair tipped over backwards, and he swallowed the toe. Sadly, [the] Toe [...] was not recovered.'

However, the club has not been short of toe donors and a series of replacement toes have been given for an array of reasons, including as result of an amputation due to an inoperable corn, frostbite, amputation due to diabetes and one even arrived in a jar of alcohol with the message, 'Don't wear open-toe sandals while mowing the lawn.'

Captain Dick came up with the original rules for the grisly sourtoe cocktail over the course of a drunken evening with friends and they were simply 'take a beer glass full of champagne, drop in the toe, tip the glass back'.Since then a number have been swallowed, lost or destroyed and the rules have changed slightly. Sourtoe can be paired with any drink, but one rule remains the same, 'You can drink it fast, you can drink it slow – but the lips have gotta touch the toe.'

On 24 August 2013 Josh Clark ordered a sourtoe shot and deliberately swallowed the toe. He promptly paid the $500 fine and exited the saloon. This was the first time the toe was deliberately consumed, but as a precautionary measure the fine was increased to $2,500.

A human toe in a cocktail proves that when it comes to drinks recipes the only limit on ingredients is the bounds of the mixologist's imagination. Some drinks are revolting by design, some have questionable production methods while others are plainly bizarre.

There is a long tradition of drinks sold with purported medicinal purposes. One such drink is snake wine, whose origins span back to China's Western Zhou dynasty. In traditional Chinese medicine distilling a snake's 'essence' into wine is considered a cure-all, capable of curing everything from impotence to hair loss and many things in between. Widely peddled as a strong aphrodisiac, snake wine is still a popular 'tonic'.

Winemakers typically incorporate one snake per bottle and add herbs, roots or even other creatures to increase the potency and healing properties of the drink. The bottle is filled with rice wine or spirit alcohol and is left to steep for a few months. Snake venom and snake blood are also mixed with alcohol to create invigorating or restorative tonics.

It is essential that great care is taken when preparing a batch of snake wine. If the reptile is not drowned properly it can remain alive and dormant in the wine for months, ready to attack whoever should dare to uncork the bottle.

A woman from China's Heilongjiang province who required hospitalisation made British headlines in 2013 after she was bitten on the hand by a snake that she had been infusing in sorghum wine for three months. One newspaper reported that, 'The woman was suffering from joint pain and put the drink together after she was given the snake by her husband, in a bid to help combat the illness. Whenever she felt her pain flare up she would pour herself a tiny shot of the shejiu (snake wine) from the large, glass decanter via a tap at the bottom. But while stirring the snake it tried to escape, biting her on the hand.' ('Woman Bit by Pit Viper Snake after Marinating it in Wine for Three Months', 2013).

There are many different versions of a *ruou thuoc* or 'medicine wine' available in Vietnam, many of which are infused with the remains of wildlife, including endangered species. These drinks are all purported to be health-giving but there is little or no scientific evidence to support such claims.

However, do not be fooled into thinking that drinks peddled as health tonics were not a known entity in Blighty; many such drinks existed. One British cure-all drink utilised the common garden snail in a recipe called 'snail water'. The snail was hailed as 'one of the cleanest feeders in the world,' (Jennifer Munroe, 2011) and the renowned herbalist Nicholas Culpeper noted that, 'the reason why they cure a consumption is this; Man being made of the slime of the earth, the slimy substance recovers him when he is wasted.' (Culpeper, 1708). During the eighteenth and nineteenth centuries snails were collected and infused into a water that could be taken as a general tonic, but most especially for the treatment of respiratory difficulties and consumption. The recipe requires a vast quantity of snails which are combined with botanicals and milk.

Snail Water
Take of comfrey and succory-roots, of each four ounces, liquorice, three ounces, the leaves of hart's-tongue, plantain, ground-ivy, red-nettle, yarrow, brooklime, watercresses, dandelion, and agrimony, of each two large handfuls; gather these herbs in dry weather, and do not wash them, but wipe them clean with a cloth. Then take

five hundred snails, cleansed from their shells, but not scoured, and of whites of eggs beaten up to a water, a pint, four nutmegs grossly beaten, the yellow rind of one lemon and one orange. Bruise all the roots and herbs and put them together, with the other ingredients, in a gallon of new milk, and a pint of Canary; let them stand close covered, forty-eight hours, and then distill them in a common still, with a gentle fire. This quantity will fill a still twice. It will keep good a year, and is best when made spring or fall; but it is best when new. You must not cork up the bottles for three months, but cover them with paper. It is immediately fit for use; take a quarter of a pint of this water, and put to it as much milk warm from the cow, and drink it in the morning, and at four o'clock in the afternoon, and fast two hours after. To take powder of crab's eyes with it, as much as will lie on a sixpence, mightily assists to sweeten the blood. When you drink this water, be very regular in your diet, and eat nothing salt nor sour.

(Lovell, 1884)

The world of drinks can be a curious one and even seemingly innocent tipples can have their dirty secrets. The question of 'do you fancy a drink' perhaps deserves careful consideration.

Chapter 9

A Country Feast

Badger hair has been used for more than two centuries to make shaving brushes, paintbrushes and even in ladies' fashion for hat trims, but what about badger for supper? The thought of a dish of roast badger may be considered bizarre in the twenty-first century, but throughout history the meat has enjoyed some popularity.

Badger doesn't appear in any of the great eighteenth-century British cookbooks, but it does crop up in some records. Today, badger isn't really on the menu, except in the case of those who cook roadkill, but this hasn't always been the case. In an article in the *Gloucestershire Echo* in 1923 entitled 'Hunting with The Cotswold Hounds' the account of the day's hunting includes the words 'We found, killed, and ate a badger.'

The late cook and author Dickson Wright testified that badger had always been a country staple, though it seems to have been a rural dish. There are tales of West Country pubs serving badger ham as a bar snack and badger meat enjoys more popularity in Europe. In France *blaireau au sang* (badger with blood) is a well-remembered dish, while Italy and the Balkans have a rural culture of badger eating. In Russia badgers have been a food and a folk-medicine for centuries and their fat is considered a cure for coughs and chest infections.

Roadkill enthusiast Arthur Boyt who lives in Cornwall has been eating animals killed by vehicles on roads for decades and even wrote a roadkill recipe book for like-minded cooks with an inclination towards a free dinner scraped off the road. Boyt is undoubtedly a connoisseur of roadkill and a creative home cook who frequently serves up dishes of badger. His recipe is simple: he skins and joints the badger, saves the offal to enjoy in other dishes and then makes a traditional casserole with vegetables in pretty much the same way you would approach beef or pork.

European recipes for badger often instruct that the badger be laid in running water for several days to get rid of the rank flavor. Boyt says that's only necessary for fox and that badger, though it doesn't need to be hung, can be treated like game and can be enjoyed and eaten when it's 'quite green'.

While Boyt has been eating various roadkill for decades he has a particularly liking for badger and despite likening labrador to lamb and having enjoyed a vast array of 'exotic' meats, his favourite snack is a badger sandwich. Mr Boyt says he is particularly partial to the badger head, which includes four distinctive tastes: the jaw muscles, salivary glands, tongue and brains. ('Fed up with Jamie? So try roadkill rat or badger', 2006).

Boyt may be considered to have a curious palate, but the wartime correspondent for *The Western Morning News* on Saturday, 22 February 1941 wrote:

> In Italy they eat the flesh of badgers, and so they do in Germany, boiling it with pears. Incidentally, badger hams were a local delicacy in parts of England less than a century ago and a badger feast – at which a roasted badger eaten with penknives, no forks being allowed – is an annual event at the Cow Inn, Ilchester. The diet of badgers is different from that of foxes; except in spring, when they eat many young rabbits, badgers do not themselves consume much flesh, and there is no reason why they should not be good to eat. They are said to taste much like pork, but travelers say that bear meat provides a closer comparison.

Recipes for badger do invariably turn up and it seems that a brock ham was once considered a good replacement for other meats.

The *Birmingham Daily Post* in 1973 reported, 'Badger meat could soon take the place of the traditional Sunday Joint', explaining that 'badger meat is said to look and taste like pork.' The article explained that due to rising meat prices 'Recently, badger meat has been advertised for sale In local papers, and if this is allowed to continue it is only a matter of time before it is sold over the counter and finds its way on to the dinner table.'

Badger certainly did find its way onto the 'sett' menu of The Butcher's Arms in Sonning Common in 1986 as part of their themed menu. Their advertisement read, 'A Taste of Old England Night: This is a three course meal costing Just £5 featuring a different dish of days gone by such as Oxford John and Aldermans Walk, two traditional lamb based dishes, and Bacon Badger.' It must be pointed out that the recipe for bacon badger doesn't contain actual badger, but perhaps this recipe offers a chance to at least say you've had badger for dinner.

If you do fancy a real roast badger ham, then it is worth noting that since 1992 it has been illegal to kill badgers in Britain, so the only way to get one for the pot will be to pick it up off the road.

Wild meats like venison, rabbit and pigeon enjoy more popularity than badger and fox, but what about hedgehog? The tradition of eating hedgehogs is one that is commonly thought of as something that accompanies sitting around campfires. The late Dr Dora Yates, a recognised gypsy scholar, gave many interviews in which she gave instructions on cooking hedgehog. She reminisced about the time she spent with a caravan touring the roads of Britain with gypsies, and revealed a recipe for roast hedgehog: 'What you do is to slit the hedgehog open and roll it in a ball of clay. You roast it in the ashes and then the prickles come off with the clay.' And the result? 'Quite delicious rather like duck.' (Dr Dora, 1969).

Dr Dora was not alone in her praise for the eating of hedgehog. A feature in the 1925 *Yorkshire Evening Post* discusses the recipe for traditional clay baked hedgehog: 'Hedgehogs are said be very good eating. Gipsy tribes consider them great delicacy. The gipsy method cooking is to roll the animal in a ball of clay and bake it. When the clay is broken the spines remain embedded in it, leaving nothing but perfectly cooked flesh, which is excellent.

It was not just the Romani who enjoyed badger. During the Second World War meat rationing there were reports of hedgehogs being offered by butchers to supplement the meat ration and that the meat was being prescribed by some country doctors. There seemed to be little aversion to the idea of hedgehog for supper with the matter being reported as 'only a case of sophisticated tastes being adapted to a centuries-old gipsy dish'. Meanwhile, in May 1950 the question of eating hedgehog was endorsed by a doctor at the British Medical Association: 'Roast hedgehogs, I hear, are being sold by village butchers and prescribed by country doctors. I have not yet been able to run down a nice fillet of hedgehog under a butcher's counter [...] The gipsy recipe is: Take a hedgehog, coat in mud and bake. A doctor at the British Medical Association who has tasted roast hedgehog tells me he can't think there is any curative value in the flesh but it might be ordered as a cheap substitute for chicken. It is very tasty, much like chicken and easily digested, he says.' ('Roast Hedgehog', 1950).

A baked hedgehog may not be to everyone's taste, and for some the thought of cooking a flea-ridden creature could be off-putting, but whether or not the thought of hedgehog tickles your tastebuds they are now a protected species so you'll need to find a squashed one on the road to cook.

Gull eggs are considered a great delicacy by some and can command high prices on restaurant menus. Larger than a chicken egg, with deep orange yolks, most agree that they are slightly salty and some say they taste fishy. The collecting of these eggs is a mysterious affair that is shrouded in secrecy. They are a fleeting treat as their collection is limited by licenses and a short season.

When thinking of gulls we tend to think of the naughty, noisy gulls that rip open rubbish bags and scavenge in bins, but these cackling gangsters are not the ones that lay the prized eggs that restaurateurs covet. The herring gull and the great black-backed gull are the ones responsible for stalking your chips and stealing your ice cream, whereas the smaller, more delicate black-headed gull is the better behaved relative whose glossy, bluish-green speckled eggs are sought after. The harvesting of their eggs has been going on for generations. Once considered a seasonal treat for those living in coastal areas and willing to navigate the treacherous cliffs to gather them, the short season makes them a speciality.

The Victorians were great fans and avidly collected the eggs. The practice became particularly widespread during the Second World War when hens' eggs were in short supply. A number of articles appeared in the local and national press regarding the harvesting of the eggs of the guillemot and the black-headed gull during wartime and in one such article the anticipated volume of egg collection is notable:

SEA GULL EGGS TO SUPPLEMENT FOOD SUPPLIES

The nation's food supplies will soon be supplemented with sea gulls' eggs. It is estimated that hundreds of thousands of these eggs will be for sale in shops the near future. A census of the number of sea gulls around the British coasts has been completed by the Ministry officials, and arrangements have been made to collect the eggs during the spring laying season. "Fisher-folk in the coastal districts have been eating these eggs for years, and they are very palatable," states Mr G. W. Temperley of Newcastle, Honorary Northern Secretary of the Natural History Society. Mr Temperley said that there are about 150,000 black-headed gulls in the Ravenglass district of Cumberland, and each hen lays two to three eggs. "The egg of the guillemot is larger, and makes generous eating," he added. These are found in large numbers on the Bempton Cliffs in Yorkshire.

('Gull Eggs', 1941)

Despite the vast numbers of gull eggs collected during the Second World War, they were in such demand that in 1947 it was announced that gull eggs were to be imported. It was reported that 'The Food Minister has agreed with the Board of Trade to importation of gull eggs from Denmark, Holland and Eire.' (*Dundee Courier*, 1947).

Today, gull eggs are not a treat for those living in coastal districts or a wartime substitute for chicken eggs but instead are featured on the menus of the best London restaurants. *New York Times* journalist Edward Schneider described a meal of gull eggs that he enjoyed at The Ivy: 'We had a terrific time, though, and ate very well indeed, including gull's eggs, simmered in their handsome mottled shells until the whites were softly firm but the startlingly red-orange yolks still very moist, and served with homemade mayonnaise and celery salt.' He goes on to explain that 'Gull's eggs have always turned up in a certain kind of very English London restaurant. They're special.'

Egg gatherers, or 'eggers' as they are known, must hold a government licence which is renewed annually and during the season they must agree to a strict timetable that means they must be off the marshes by 9.00am Monday to Friday and by 11.00am at the weekends. Unsurprisingly, therefore, gull egg supplies are limited and expensive. These eggers have a long history of collecting gull eggs and they know their craft well, but because this is a lucrative trade many eggs are collected illegally. Poachers often don't have the experience of the licenced eggers and mistake the black-headed gulls' eggs for those of the Mediterranean gull which is a protected species. There is also the concern that many of the eggs being illegal collected and sold may not be safe for human consumption.

This rare delicacy has claimed its fair share of victims, who have fallen to their death while climbing perilous cliffs to collect the precious eggs. As far as country fare goes roadkill seems less risky to harvest, though historically a dish of rook pie or casserole would have been more likely. Most people are familiar with the nursery rhyme *Sing a song of sixpence* from childhood, but rooks are is widely thought to be the pie filling in question rather than the popular garden songster. The 'black birds' are thought to be actually young rooks.

Rook pie for some was considered an excellent dish, but there also existed a degree of distaste, distrust and snobbery for the 'free food'. *The Cassell's Dictionary of Cookery* (1883) says, 'the rook affords a dry and coarse meat. A pie made of young rooks is tolerable; at least, it is the best form for using these birds for food.'

In June 1885 Leadenhall Market in London was described as being 'black with young rooks'. These birds, which originated mainly from the West of England and Scotland, were being sold cheaply ' for few pence apiece the market'. The *Paisley Herald and Renfrewshire Advertiser* (1875) tackled the issue of whether the rooks were 'worth buying and eating at the price.' The author was not 'very enthusiastic to their merits', explaining that they were cheap but then their preparation requires 'considerable trouble' for 'a few morsels' of meat. The preparation of the birds does appear fiddly and only the breasts were considered worthy of eating, though it seems that it may not have been just the palaver of preparing the birds that was the issue as much as the appearance: 'rooks when dead are most unpresentable birds, and not at all suggestive of savoury pies; and hence perhaps the prejudice against them.' Many accounts have likened the rook to pigeon concluding, 'rook pie is good as pigeon pie,' but for some the idea of rook pie remained unappealing and the big selling point seems to have been their low cost.

It is certain that many accounts of rook meat compare it favourably to pigeon and that because it was so cheap and abundant during the season it simply got passed off as pigeon in pies. An account from 1929 warns 'do not be surprised if you get young rook served pie nominally called pigeon on the menu. Indeed I have tasted rook pie that might easily have passed for genuine pigeon.' ('Pigeon Pie – or It May be Rook', 1929). Some accounts of rook are positively glowing, including one from the 1980s in which the breast meat is commended:

The deep plump breasts, more tender than the youngest chicken, make delicious eating when the cook knows her jot. Old racing men years ago (and possibly still) used talk about the high-class restaurant for owners and trainers at the Goodwood May meeting in Hampshire where the speciality would always be rook pie and if anyone turned his nose up at it he would be regarded as a nobody from nowhere. Naturally after such a meal if somebody asked you what you had for lunch you didn't say "Crows". Then there is the wood-quiet or wild pigeon, a menace to the village farmer, but from the flesh of this bird, which was never more plentiful in living memory, an excellent dish can be made called pigeon-pie, the recipe for which can be found in any good cookery book. These birds used to be caught with nets in large numbers during the harvest season and sold in poultry and game shops.'

('Rook Pie', 1980)

It seems universally accepted that the preparation of rooks is fiddly and that the bitter tasting spine should be removed, but as to whether they were good to eat was, it seems, all a matter of taste and it certainly never became a mainstay dish. It is certain that rook pie was a farmhouse recipe and in rural communities was considered a welcome treat. The following advice was given: 'Never make the old birds into pies – and the young ones only when very young. Do not pluck the birds – skin them. This is quickly done If the head and lower part of the legs are first removed and the wings are cut off at the middle Joint.' (Rook Pie, 1935). Rook pie was often paired with stewing steak and gravy for hot pies and boiled eggs and jelly to make a cold cutting pie.

Rook shooting was once a traditional part of the country calendar, but organised rook shooting is now a thing of the past. It is illegal to shoot rooks in Britain except when they pose a problem to agriculture, other wildlife, or public health. Rook pie is now a rarity and for the most part merely a nostalgic food memory. The days when articles appeared in the local press crowing 'ROOK PIE TO APPEAR' have certainly gone and it seems there will never again be announcements that read 'Lovers of rook pie will glad hear that the birds have made their appearance this week-end, and are now being offered at 1s 3d.to 1s 6d. the half-dozen.' (*Yorkshire Evening Post*, 1912). Now these birds have been elevated to the status of 'delicacy' or 'curiosity' on account of their rarity. While historically widely consumed, they were never considered a food for top tables and seem to have remained as a countryman's dish. In 1951 Mr Roosevelt Wilkinson of Louth, one of the county's biggest poultry dealers, said 'We sell rooks at this season in hundreds but only Lincolnshire motile will buy them. The townsman has never heard of rook pie and does not know a delicacy it is.'

Young rooks, referred to as 'branchers' because they hop around on the branches, were shot in the vicinity of the nest and their meat was mainly made into pies, sometimes quite elaborate ones: 'Mrs Yates is known over a wide area for the excellence of her catering. One of her most vivid memories of bygone days is the local Foresters jubilee dinner, held in Church House in May 1913, for which she made an enormous rook pie which had to be cooked in the village bakehouse. A hundred rooks, 25lb of steak, and six dozen hard boiled eggs, jellied down with pigs trotters, made up the ingredients, and 137 guests each had portion.' ('Rook Pie', 1951). Most rook pies were not of the huge proportion of Mrs Yates' and a more modest recipe appears in Mrs Beeton's *Poultry and Game* book. Her recipe to serve five or six people requires, six young rooks, 3/4 lb of rump steak and hot stock to be encased in pastry. (Beeton, 1926).

In 1911 the objections to rook are challenged and a valiant defence of the meat is offered in *The Pall Mall Gazette*:

> Some people are shy of rook pie because this bird is closely allied to and commonly confounded with the

carrion-crow. We recommend that any such prejudice be at once discarded for ever. There is also another absurd belief that rook let is the most indigestible meat; indeed, I have seen the respective merits and dements of certain game meats tabulated follows: Rooks require six hours digest, pigeons three hours and ten minutes, pheasants five minutes less, grouse two and half hours, snipe and larks two hours, venison one and half hours, and boiled tripe one hour. This table is supposed to establish the worst possible position for rook-pie in a gustatory sense but remain a bit sceptical the compiler's authority. As matter of fact, rook pie is, or ought to be, as easily digested as pigeon pie, to which it not inferior. Everything depends on the cook. But rook pie has not yet reached such a plebeian level that the country cottage-woman would be at the trouble to make one, even if she knew how, and could get hold of such aristocratic game with rectory or "'hall" mark on it.

('Rook Shooting and Rook Pie', 1911)

Rook-eating fanatics have throughout the ages waxed lyrical about the benefits of a good rook pie but though the dish seems to have suffered from a long term image problem in 2007 Gordon Ramsay earned rook meat a headline when he made a rook salad and said 'I think it is about time something like this found its way back on to traditional British menus.' In this instance the historic dish made the headlines for all the wrong reasons. The emphasis was on offences under the Wildlife and Countryside Act 1981 having been committed rather than the merit of rooks for eating. Similarly, when in 2011 an Isle of Wight restaurant served up a dish that included fledgling rook it was swiftly removed when it was discovered the birds had been illegally shot. Again rook made the headlines, but not for the eating. It seems that rook is now off British menus and there is no point cawing about it.

Chapter 10

Perils and Pearls

Female epicure: "OH, MISTER, I'M SURE THAT WAS A BAD ONE!"

Oyster salesman (indignantly): "WHAT D'YER MEAN? THEN YOU SHOULDN'T 'A' SWALLERED IT, MUM! I'VE BEEN IN THIS TRADE A MATTER O' TEN YEARS, AND NEVER."

Lady: "WELL, IT CERTAINLY LEFT A NASTY TASTE."

Salesman (mollified): "WELL, THERE'S NO DENYIN' THAT SOME OF 'EM IS 'IGHER IN FLAVIOUR THAN OTHERS!"

(*A Soft Answer &c*, 1879)

Today, oysters are considered a decadent and luxurious food; the perfect companion to champagne. These slippery customers are generally eaten raw with a squeeze of fresh lemon juice, sometimes a dash of tabasco sauce, or popped into an oyster martini.

While oysters grace the menus of the UK's finest seafood restaurants and there are festivals dedicated to sampling the delicacy, some people can find them somewhat intimidating. The look of an oyster can be off putting for some, while the thought of its slippery texture and oceanic flavour is enough to make others coil in revulsion.

To eat an oyster properly you should tip the whole thing into your mouth straight from the shell and you should always chew it a few times to release the full mineral-laden flavours. They are not something that should be thrown down the throat like a shot. If oysters are 'milky' then novices might have a surprise. The white colouring that lends to an oyster being termed 'milky' occurs when they are getting ready to spawn and when you bite into them they will coat your mouth and give an unusual feel. As Jonathon Swift said, 'It was a bold man that first ate on oyster.' Swift had borrowed this sentiment from Thomas Fuller's *Worthies of England* which was published in 1662, 'He was a very valiant man who first adventured on eating of oysters.' Indeed, eating oyster does require a certain degree of bravery, not just because of their strange looks, acquired texture and taste, but because of the risks of poisoning and even death that oysters can potentially spell.

Prior to the Romans arrival in Britain in 43AD, shellfish was seen as second-rate in comparison to meat and fish in so much as it was something for consumption when other options did not avail. The Romans, however, had a great enthusiasm for eating all the fruits of the sea and demand for shellfish, including oysters, whelks, cockles, mussels and limpets, grew.

During the Roman occupation the oyster was a popular dish dressed with herbs, egg yolks and fermented fish sauce, but when the Romans left and the Romano-British town and villa way of life faded, it lost its status as a delicacy as people lost their taste for them.

When it comes to fashion, it is a commonly held belief that nothing is ever new, and the same could be applied to culinary fashion. While the tradition of oyster eating fell from grace for a few centuries, by the eighth century oysters were back on the menu and by the 1400s it was a popular source of nutrition.

Fish and shellfish became important in Medieval Europe because the imposition of 'fish days' by the Church. This meant that regardless of class or status the consumption of the flesh of animals was forbidden on Fridays and Saturdays until the late Middle Ages. Wednesdays were also observed as fish days until the early fifteenth century. In addition to the fish days that were imposed on a weekly basis, further fish days were to be observed during the six weeks of Lent and on other special religious days. These rules were strictly enforced and while the classification of fish was stretched to include beavers, seals, frogs and the barnacle goose, oysters were an extremely popular choice, in addition to freshwater fish, herring and cod.

The medieval medical lore that forbade the mixing of fish and meat in the same meal influenced the way in which oysters were enjoyed, so much so that it was not until the seventeenth century that they began to be cooked with roast capon, beef or duck. With the rules that had dominated previous centuries relaxed, oysters were suddenly made into stuffings, sauces, sausages and pies. While still enjoyed on their own and as an hors d'oeuvre, they were now enjoying popularity raw, stewed, pureed, spiced, roasted and baked.

During the eighteenth century green oysters became popular. In the shallow waters off the island of Mersea in Essex the oysters native to Britain, with their distinctive flat shells, developed green beards of harmless algae in September. Legend has it that Colchester's native oysters were described by the Romans as the only good thing to come out of Britain, but they now enjoyed great popularity with Britons themselves.

Local purveyors collected the green oysters and put them into pits dug in the saltmarshes for six to eight weeks, turning them a deep dark green, which was much admired in London and was the height of culinary fashion.

The abundant use of oysters continued into the Victorian period, but far from being a delicacy of the privileged few, pickled oysters were a fast and portable food for the poorer classes. Oysters were peddled by costermongers and Charles Dickens' character Sam Weller remarks, 'Poverty and oysters always seem to go together.'

The London Illustrated News described the scene of 'oyster-day', otherwise known as 'the day on which oysters are first brought into the London market at Billingsgate.' This occasion is described as being a 'sort of festival in the streets' and from the description it is clearly a popular and eventful time: 'The Oyster-day has arrived and a very busy day it usually proves; for Mr. Mayhew, in his

"London Labour and the Poor," tells us that "the number of oysters sold by the costermongers amounts to 124,000,000 a year. These, at four a penny, would realise the large sum of £129,650. We may, therefore, safely assume that £125,000 is spent yearly in oysters in the streets of London." ('Oyster Day', 1851).

The cry of the costermonger was a familiar sound of the street as they hawked their wares, and no doubt none was more popular than the cry ''Oysters, a penny a lot'. (Mayhew, 1851). The cheap price of oysters and their popularity as a staple food meant that by the middle of the nineteenth century, oysters and scallops were being dredged in huge numbers all along the Sussex coast by fleets of oyster smacks. Suddenly the natural oyster beds became exhausted, partially through overfishing and partially through pollution. The future of the oyster looked quite bleak for a time and it was only through the deliberate artificial breeding that they were saved from extinction.

The oyster was prized as the easiest and the simplest of meals, often served with a dash of vinegar, a sprinkling of pepper with bread and butter, as was reflected by Lewis Carroll:

> A loaf of bread, the Walrus said,
> Is what we chiefly need:
> Pepper and vinegar besides
> Are very good indeed –
> Now if you're ready, Oysters, dear,
> We can begin to feed!

(Carroll, 1871)

As the seemingly insatiable appetite for oysters continued, English oyster farmers established artificial oyster beds, or ponds as they were called, and developed a good trade in keeping up with the demand. The two prominent figures in oyster farming in Emsworth, near Portsmouth, were J. D. Foster and John Kennett who bought up most of the oyster beds in the area.

Oysters continued to appear regularly on British menus and were used as a cheap bulking agent in dishes such as steak pie. However, the oyster empire was about to be severely shaken when in the early 1900s council workers relaid a number of the sewers and drains which emptied onto the Emsworth foreshore. Mr Foster had constructed a number of new ponds in close proximity to the outflow and had seeded them with a considerable quantity of young oysters. Unfortunately, the significance of the relaying of sewerage pipes was not immediately recognised and the risk of mollusc contamination was not considered.

Unbeknownst to him, Foster's oysters had been contaminated by the foreshore outflow, and so in 1902 scandal broke when he supplied oysters to the local mayoral banquet and several of the diners, including the Dean of Winchester, died of typhoid. Stories reporting the death of the Earl of Winchester were in all the newspapers days before Christmas and the articles did not inspire seasonal feasting on oysters:

> SUSPECTED OYSTER POISONING
> We regret to learn that the Dean of Winchester, the Very Rev. W. R. W. Stephens, died shortly after nine o'clock yesterday evening. He had been suffering from typhoid fever, contracted, it is believed, through eating contaminated oysters at the Mayoral banquet Winchester on the 11th. The Dean was present at the banquet to the ex-Mayor and is said have eaten some the oysters to which is attributed the outbreak typhoid fever in Hampshire. Dr. Stephens was one of the first attacked, and his death is the third in Winchester recorded in connection with the epidemic. He had a serious relapse on Sunday morning, and as no hope was entertained of his recovery all the members his family were summoned.
>
> ('Death of Earl of Winchester', 1902)

The lucrative Emsworth oyster empire collapsed almost overnight and the town, where so many relied upon the oyster trade for their living, was destroyed by the damning finding that the deaths were the result of contaminated oysters.

A number of emergency meetings were called to discuss the problem of oyster contamination and to call for the practice of pumping raw sewerage in the vicinity of oyster ponds to stop. These were of such importance that they were reported nationally in the press:

> OYSTER POISONING. MERCHANTS TAKE ACTION
> At meeting of the committee of Oyster Merchants the Fishmongers' Hall, London, yesterday a resolution was adopted recommending that merchants and oyster planters requested to advise the committee of any discharge of sewage occurring in the neighbourhood of their fisheries, in order that measures should be taken to guard against any contamination. A further resolution was adopted calling for a conference of those interested in oyster culture to protest against the discharge of sewage into rivers and estuaries.
>
> ('Oyster Poisoning', 1902)

The words 'oyster poisoning' were now a common headline and public confidence continued to be rocked as more reports of contaminated oysters came out. Details of oysters contaminated with sewerage, which Dr Kliez, the city bacteriologist had condemned as unfit for consumption, were still being brought from a bed close by ('Contaminated Oysters', 1903) and this did nothing to help the ailing industry. Stories of polluted oysters kept trickling in and five years after the death of the Dean of Winchester reports of contaminated oysters being sold were still surfacing:

POLLUTED OYSTERS
William Bartlett, oyster merchant of Wivenhoe, was
fined £20 and costs at Colchester on Saturday for selling
oysters which, according to the evidence of Dr Kliez of
St. Bartholomew's Hospital, were polluted with sewage.

('Polluted Oysters', 1907)

Foster made a claim for damages against Warblington Council for
£1,500, later increasing to £18,000 after several years of increasingly
acrimonious litigation. In 1906 his rival oyster farmer, Kennett,
testified that Foster had not only known about the sewerage outflow
but had deliberately put his beds in that area to make use of the extra
nutrients in the water. Foster's award was reduced accordingly, but the
impact on the oyster trade continued to be felt.

While sewerage beds were to blame for the mayoral dinner oyster
poisonings in 1902, the reality is that a dish of oysters can be a risky
business and food poisoning is not uncommon, even without the help
of raw sewerage. Oysters are filter feeders, meaning that they eat by
constantly drawing in water and materials in the water they inhabit,
including harmful bacteria and viruses. These bacteria and viruses
can become concentrated in an oyster's body and infect people who
eat them raw or undercooked. In live oysters there are two pathogenic
viruses, norovirus and vibrio. Norovirus can cause intestinal
inflammation or gastritis, while vibrio is a bacterium that causes
cholera and has symptoms such as high fever, shock, blistering, and
even death from blood infection.

Unlike, many other foods that are unsafe or unfit for human
consumption, an oyster that contains harmful bacteria does not look,
smell, or even taste different from any other, so until the effects of
illness grip the unsuspecting diner, the oyster's victim will usually be
oblivious to the harmful nature of their shellfish dinner.

It is certain that despite the risks of sickness, stroke or even death
oysters are not as risky as the delicacy known as blood cockles or

blood clams which are known to carry the viruses of hepatitis A, typhoid and dysentery. In 1988 thirty-one people died from eating these clams and it is reported that fifteen per cent of people who consume blood clams gain some sort of infection. Boiling these shellfish does not prevent the presence of the deadly pathogens and so dysentery is a very real possibility.

While the blood clam does make the oyster look like a much safer option, oyster eating is the culinary equivalent of Russian roulette and so when dining on oysters it is worth considering splashing out on the good champagne, for you never know whether it will be your last supper.

References

$10,000 Reward for Two Fresh Eggs. (1915, Jun 06). *Evening star (Washington, D.C.)*.

(1880, Nov 27). *North Wilts Herald*, p. 2.

(1897, Mar 25). *Flintshire Observer Mining Journal and General Advertiser for the Counties of Flint Denbigh*.

(1931, Jul 30). *Aberdeen Press and Journal*.

(1947, Mar 11). *Dundee Courier*.

(1972, Jul 18). *Belfast Telegraph*.

(1978, Aug 1). *New York Times*, pp. Section A, Page 4.

(1997, Aug 3). *Sunday Mirror*.

(1998, Feb 6). *Irish Independent*.

(2017, Aug 20). *The Sunday Times*.

(2018, Jan 27). *The Guardian*.

A Frog Farm. (1896, Aug 8). *The South Wales Daily Post*.

'A Taste of Old England Night'. (1986, Sep 19). *Reading Evening Post*.

Acton, E. (1845). *Modern Cookery for Private Families*.

American Frog Farming. (1894, Dec 8th). *South Wales Daily News*.

Appert, N. (n.d.). *Le livre de tous les ménages ou l'art de conserver pendant plusieurs années toutesles substances animales ou végétales; Barrois l'aine:*.

Association, B. M. (1909). *Secret Remedies: What They Cost & What They Contain*. London.

Baby's Toes Brawn. (1906, Sep 22). *Weekly Mail*.

Badger meat could soon take the place of the traditional Sunday Joint. (1973, May 11). *Birmingham Daily Post*.

Barbier, J. (1994). *Nicholas Appert Inventeur et humaniste*. Paris: CCB Royer, Saga Sciences.

Beef Tea for the Million. (1907, Nov 29). *Carnavon and Denbigh Herald and North and South Wales Independant.*

Beeton, I. (1861). *Mrs Beeton's Book of Household Management.* London: Ward Lock & Bowden Ltd.

Beeton, I. (1861). *Mrs Beeton's Book of Household Managemment.*

Beeton, I. (1865). *Mrs Beeton's Every Day Cookery and Housekeeping Book.*

Beeton, I. (1895). *Mrs Beeton's Book of Household Management.* London: Ward, Lock & Bowden Ltd.

Bell, M. E. (2006). *Vampires and Death in New England, 1784 to 1892, Anthropology and Humanism* (Vol. 31 issue 2).

Bristles in Brawn. (1910, Jun 30). *The Welsh Coast Pioneer and Review for North Cambria.*

Brothers, D. (1882). *The Cosmopolitan Cook and Recipe book.* Buffalo NY.

Bryder, L. (1988). *Below th Magic Mountain: A Social History of Tuberculosis in Twentieth Century Britian.* New York: Oxford University Press.

Buckmaster, J. C. (1874). *Buckmaster's Cookery.* London: George Routledge and Sons.

Byron, M. (1914). *The British Home Cookery Book.*

Caporael, L. R. (1976, Apr 2). Ergotism: The Satan Loosed in Salem? *Science, 192.*

Chester Tripe Dresser Summonsed. (1901, Jul 3). *The Chester Courant And Advertiser for North Wales.*

Chitterling Song. (1971).

Choked by Tripe. (1889, May 7). *South Wales Echo.*

Christmas Display. (1910, Dec 24). *Denbighshire Free Press.*

Cookman, s. (2000). *Ice Blink: The Tragic Fate of Sir John Franklin's Lost Polar Expedition.* New York: John Wiley & Sons.

Culpeper, N. (1708). *Pharnacopoeia Londinensis: or the London Dispensatory.* London.

Dangers of Tinned Food. (1897, Jul 28). *South Wales Daily News (3rd edition).*

Day, C. A. (2017). *Consumptive Chic: A History of Beauty, Fashion, and disease.* London: Bloomsbury Academic.

Deadly Brawn. (1908, May 30). *Cardiff Times.*

Death After Eating Brawn. (1908, Jun 6). *Weekly News.*

Decayed Food. (1905, Feb 17). *Barry Herald.*

Department of Agriculture. (1954). *Bullfrog Farming and Frogging in Florida.*

Department of Conservation of State of Louisiana. (1933). *Bulletin.*

Dictionarium Domesticum. (1736). London: Hitch, Davis, Austen.

Diseased Meat as Brawn. (1906, Aug 4). *Evening Express (Special Edition).*

Dr Dora. (1969, Nov 26). *Liverpool Echo.*

Drinking Blood. (1879, Oct 8). *Aberdeen Evening Express.*

English Frog Preserves. (1888, May 26). *South Wales Echo.*

Everard, H. (1935). *J & E Hall Ltd 1785-1935.*

Fadda et al., F. e., Hoz, O. A., & Puolanne, P.-K. A. (2008). *Principles of Meat Fermentation.* University of Hellsinki.

Farmers Bulletin. (1921). *Farmers Bulletin 1186 Pork on the Farm, Killing. Curing & Canning,* 8.

Fed up with Jamie? So try roadkill rat or badger. (2006, Jan 31). *The Times.*

Feeding on Beef Blood. (1885, Mar 22). *Rocky Mountain News.*

For Women Folk I HOMELY HINTS AND DAINTY DISHES. (1906, Oct 25). *Evening Express.*

Forbes, e. a. (n.d.). *Microscopic Post-Mortem Changes: the Chemistry of Decomposition.* 2017.

Francatelli, C. E. (1852). *A Plain Cookery Book for the Working Classes.*

Frog Eating and Frog Farming. (1900, Jul 5). *Flintshire Observer Mining Journal and General Advertiser.*

Frog Eating in England. (1899, Jan 13). *Barry Herald.*

Frog Eating New-Yorkers. (1909, Apr 19). *Evening Express.*

Frozen Meat. (1882, Jun 23). *The Cambrian.*

Fuller, E. (1999). *The Great Auk: The Extinction of the Original Penguin.* Bunker Hill Publishing.

Ginger Beer Plant. (1980, Oct 29). *Belfast Telegraph.*

Glasse, H. (1793). *The Art of Cookery Made Plain and Easy.*

Gull Eggs. (1941, Mar 1). *Hartlepool Northern Dail Mail.*

Hedgehog. (1925, Aug 20). *Yorkshire Evening Post.*

Hedgehog. (1950, May 24). *Halifax Evening Courier.*

How To Make Calfs Foot Jelly. (1887, Jan 8th). *Cardiff Times.*

Hunting with the Cotswold Hounds. (1923, Oct 11). *Gloucestershire Echo.*

International Tin Research & Development Council. (1939). *Historic Tinned Food.*

International Tin Research & Development Council. (1939). *Historic Tinned Food, Publication No 85.*

J.A Harvie- Brown, T. B. (1888). *Vertebrate Fauna of the Outer Hebrides.*

Jelly that Jells. (1896, Sep 19). *The Cardiff Times.*

Jennifer Munroe, R. L. (2011). *Ecofeminist Approaches to Early Modernity.* New York.

k., B. (2011). *Tuberculosis and the Victorian Literary Imagination.* Cambridge: Cambridge University Press.

Kay Shuttleworth, S. J. (1832). *The Moral and physical condition of the working classes employed in cotton manufacture in Manchester.*

Keenleyside, A. (1997). The Final Days of the Franklin Expedition - New Skeletal Evidence. *Artic Magazine*, 50:1.

Kelly, M. (1823). *Good Things In England.* (F. White, Ed.)

Kowal W, B. O. (1991). *Source Indentification of Lead found in tissues of sailors from the Franklin Artic Expedition of 1845.* J Archelog Sci.

Labouchère, H. (1871). *Diary of the Beseiged Resident in Paris.* London: Hurst and Blackett.

Lee, N. (1854). *The Cooks Own Book, And Housekeeper's Register.* C.S. Francis and Co.

Leon P.A.M, C. H. (2015). *The Morphology of the Thirioux dodos.*

Letter of the Conseil de Santé to General Caffarelli, préfet maritime. (1803, Nov).

Lovell, M. S. (1884). *The Edible Mollusca Of Great Britain And Ireland, 1884)*. London: L Reeve & Co.

M.D., W. H. (1876). *Theraputics of Tuberculosis or Pulmonary Consumption*. New York: Boericke and Tafel.

Manufacture of Brawn. (1885, Mar 11). *South Wales Echo*.

Markham, G. (1615). *English Huswife*. London.

Marlow, F. (2010). *The Hadza: Hunter-Gatherers of Tanzania (Volume 3)*. University of California Press.

Martin, A. (1807, May 22). *Letter of Admiral Martin, préfet maritime (navy chief administrator), to the "Ministre de laMarine*.

May, R. (1660). The Accomplisht Cook.

May, R. (1660). *The Accomplisht Cook.*

McCoogan, K. (2001). *Fatal Passage: The Story of John Rae, the Artic Hero Time Forgot*. New York: Carroll & Graf.

Michel, A. (1871)., *Le Siège de Paris, 1870-71*. Paris: Librairie A. Courcier.

(1999). *Ministero delle politiche agricole alimentari e forestali for Italy*. MINISTRY OF AGRICULTURAL, FOOD AND FOREST POLICIES, del decreto ministriale.

Mitchell, M. H. (1935). *The Passenger Pigeon in Ontario*. Toronto: The University of Toronto Press.

Money in Frog Farming. (1902, Jun 27). *Evening Express*.

Montagen, P. (2001). *Larousse Gastronomique:The Worlds Greatest Cookery Encylopedia*. Hamlin.

Mrs Beeton's Book of Houshold Management. (1880). London.

Nathan Sheppard. (1871). *Shut Up in Paris*. London: Richard Bentley & Son.

Old Testament, Leviticus 11:47. (n.d.).

Parmentier, A. (1810). *Cadet de Vaux A. Examen des produits conserves par Monsieur Nicolas Appert*. Bull, Pharmacie.

Passenger Pigeon. (1915, Jun 6). *Evening star (Washington, D.C.)*.

Paterson, C. D. (1998). *The Two Fat Ladies, Full Throttle*. New York: Clarkson Potter.

Pepys, S. (1957). *Selections from the diary of Samuel Pepys 1660-1669.* New York: Fine Editions Press.

Pigeons. (1843, Apr 29). *Niles (Michigan) Republican (NR).*

Pliny. (1982). *Naturalis Historia : Pliny the Elder.* (J. I. Whalley, Ed.) Victoria and Albert Museum.

Plumbtre, A. (1813). *Domestic Management: or The Healthful Cookery Book London.* B and R Crosby and Co.

Poisoned by Tinned Lobster. (1897, Oct 12). *South Wales Echo.*

Pools of Blood. (2019, Jun 29). *The Sun.*

Ptomaine Poisoning: Caution to Hotel Keepers. (1900, Mar 31). *South Wales Daily News.*

Quinn, A. H. (1998). *Edgar Allan Poe: A Critcal Biography.* Baltimore: The John Hopkins University Press.

Randolph, M. (1848). *The Virginia Housewife or Methodical Cook.* Philadelphia: E.H. Butler & Co.

Rats in the Cider Vat. (1902, Oct 22). *St James Gazette.*

Rebecca L. Spang, (2002). *"And they ate the zoo": Relating gastronomic exoticism in the siege of Paris,' Modern Language Notes, 107 (September 1992), 752-73; Hollis Clayson, Paris in Despair: Art and Everyday Life under Siege, 1870-71.* University of Chicago Press.

Richard Sykes Advert. (1910, Sep 17). *Rhyl Journal.*

Roast Hedgehog. (1950, May 25). *Belfast Telegraph.*

Salt, H. (1886). *A Plea for Vegetarianism and Other Essays.* The Vegetarian Society.

Seizure of tinned food. (1899, Apr 8). *Rhyl Journal.*

Silverman, K. (1991). *Edgar Allan Poe: A Mournful and Never-Ending Rememberance.* New York: Harper Perenial.

Slater, F. (2016). *From Black to Green: Midlands to Mid-Wales (& The World) Through a Countryman's Eyes.*

Smith, A. B. (1984). *The invisible Whale.*

Society, A. A.-O. (1969). *Yesterday's Shopping, the reprinted catalogue of the Army & Navy Stores: 1907.* Newton Abbot: David Charles.

Soyer, A. (1854). *Shilling Cookery for the People.*

The Best Beef Tea. (1910, Jul 16). *Denbighshire Free Press.*

The Primal Diet: The Silliest Diet Ever. (2009, Mar 21). *The Times.*

Unsound Tinned Food. (1900, Jun 2). *County Observer and Monmouthshire Central Advertiser.*

Unwholesome Brawn. (1886, Sep 4th).

Walker, J. (1819). *Pantologia: A New Cabinet Encyclopaedia.* London.

Watson, D. C. (1915). *Food & Feeding in Health and Disease.* McAinsh & Co.

Weir, A. (1999). *Eleanor of Aquitaine: by the wrath of God, Queen of England.* Pimlico.

Woman Choked by Tripe. (1895, Oct 15). *Evening Express (pink).*

Yulin Meat Festival. (2020, Jun 19). *The Telegraph.*

Zdor, K. &. (2003). *Changes in Soviet and Post-Soviet Indigenous Diets.* Universite Laval.